T0161470

AMONG THE GREATEST

MAKE THE DECISION TO CHANGE YOUR LIFE ONE STEP AT A TIME

JOSHUA WHITE

Clovercroft Publishing

Among the Greatest: Make the Decision To
Change Your Life One Step At a Time

© 2022 by Joshua White

Published by Clovercroft Publishing, Franklin, Tennessee

Edited by Bob Irvin and OnFire Books

Cover design by Debbie Manning Sheppard

Author photo by Tyler Lizenby www.lizenbyphoto.com

Interior design by Suzanne Lawing

Printed in the United States of America

978-1-954437-3-26

To Jackson and Hendrix: humility, my sons.

With love,
Bruh

CONTENTS

INTRODUCTION

Adversity

How do you see the light at the end of the tunnel when you can't see any light at all? I guess it depends on where you are in your journey, but this is a question men have asked since the days of Socrates and Aristotle.

How can I overcome the challenges set before me to become an even greater version of myself? When I started this journey, I wasn't thinking about anything except the way my mentors had changed me, saved me, helped me. If you don't have a mentor, you have to find one. This book is about survival: survive the day, survive the elements, survive the obstacles—survive the chaos of everyday life. This has been my war. One truth I want anyone reading this book to know is that you will have enemies, people who want to see your defeat. To be an effective agent of change, you cannot let a person, or period of time, or struggle—basically, the enemy—defeat you. There will be times you have to fight through anxiety and barriers and depression even if it means living within a prolonged period of struggle. Those types of scenarios are teaching you a form of resilience which will, in turn, help you learn to live the fullest life available.

Your body begins to learn, and adapt to your surroundings, and each step you take creates a new opportunity for confidence and faith. My decision to join the Marines was bold and helped me break those emotional boundaries and gain confidence. The Marine Corps allowed me to travel and see the world, to find myself, if you will. To discover a sort of depth I had never experienced before. It also tasked me with fighting a war, one that involved invading a country as a ground troop. A war I believed in and supported my country in serving, and no one, not even my mom, could change my mind. I soon learned that no one becomes a United States Marine without going through the process of earning it.

Oddly enough, as I write this book, the sometimes-mandatory lockdowns and quarantines of 2020 during the global pandemic brought back a familiar muscle memory one would get during deployment. The isolation and time away weren't as stressful as they could have been. My mind, body, and spirit had already been conditioned—built, if you will—to withstand periods of time without loved ones. Fear and anxiety of the unknown. Why? At the ripe age of nineteen I had already experienced a lifetime of stressors.

One could even say I found myself studying abroad. The year was 2003, and I was in the middle of the desert in a foreign land far from my family. Not knowing if I'd come back whole, or at all, was a source of stress I will never entirely shake. While I was deployed, a specific Scripture stood out to me:

"Greater love hath no man than this, that a man lay down his life for his friends" (John 15:13, KJV).

Those words were powerful and, after reading them, it occurred to me that the greatest sacrifice one could give is living for others. That, my friends, is service. That is the greatest love. But those sacrifices have lasting consequences.

You eventually pay a price for the toughness. A harsh reality is we are losing roughly twenty-two veterans each day to suicide. This weighs on me in a unique way as I understand that type of pain and hopelessness. I understand why they chose to give up. It's a balance between being self-aware and understanding that too much thinking creates overthinking. Sometimes we just need people to understand why we came back different—and a simple gesture of just being there is all the security we need. There's a reason why battle buddies are so important: when the dust settles and you are left with that feeling of aloneness, that is the greatest adversary of all.

When you're tiptoeing on the line of death, so to speak, you find out who you are as a person. And even through the dark days, I knew I had to change my life course. When I returned home from Iraq, I was clearly different. My loved ones recognized that and gave me space. I chose to move from my mother's house and chart a new path. I wanted to start college without any other distractions.

The problem was, I wasn't ready for it. I found myself fearing things, little things like going to class. Obsessively analyzing and overthinking things. I couldn't turn off the negative. It hindered my ability to live with my friend, who was simply enjoying his youth. At college, kids would come in the classroom and simply drop books on a desk. That slamming noise would startle me to the point that my heart rate would rapidly increase as if I were in a fight-or-flight situation. With things around me slowly deteriorating, I began to isolate myself in my room. I was failing school miserably, and with that I lost the means of support to live on my own. At first I wouldn't eat as much; I'd maybe go home to see my parents for some healthy food. Then it got to the point that I needed gas money, so I sold my possessions. I was broke, but my spirit wouldn't allow me to break. I didn't want to burden my parents. They had worked hard their entire life, and I needed to sustain myself. The option of going full-time in the Marines crossed my mind—a lot. It was the only constant during that period.

Instead I challenged myself to find a job outside my comfort zone. I started working at an electronics store of all places. What I haven't said yet is that crowds of people were a challenge for me. Post-Traumatic Stress Disorder (PTSD) is mysterious in that way. Even when the war is over, there are still other battles to fight. Sometimes that war is inside of you, tucked away deeply in the dark recesses of your mind. Sometimes the war is external and palpable. Either way you've got to know how and when to fight. Forcing myself back to work and engaging with complete strangers offered a form of therapy. They used to play a jingle on loop—*"Just what I needed"*—and those words couldn't have been more true. That electronics store was exactly what I needed. I needed to interact with human beings again, to not look at them as a threat. Those strangers, those people, were a part of something bigger for me, even if I didn't realize it at the time.

Another common theme you will notice in this book is that I want to pay respect to important people in my life, those who have made a difference. One is Jim. Jim was a wise old man who taught me so much about quality over quantity. You see, it doesn't matter where you come from, or how much money you have or don't, quality will *always* trump quantity. I feel sorry for those who never get a chance to meet their mentor. Jim? He taught me early on that you have to muster up the courage to take on something new. Perseverance was his favorite word. Learning how to move through your obstacles, improvising to the surroundings, and most importantly adapting to achieve the desired outcome. From the moment I met Jim I could tell he was as tough as they come. His upbringing was vastly different from mine. As a child he grew up during the Great Depression. He would often speak of how poor everyone was during those times. There simply were no jobs. Folks were doing whatever it took just to survive the day. In Jim's teenage years America was in the midst of the Second World War. Jim, like most young men his age, was called to fight. He was trained as a tail gunner on the B-24 Bomber.

Jim was a master storyteller. To sit and listen to him, it was almost as if I was transported back in time with him living out the stories. There was a time during the war, he said, when the engine would stall and there would be huge drops while he was sitting in the belly of that plane. To say he was scared was an understatement.

Jane, Jim's wife, used to say that Jim "hung the moon." Anyone who ever met him would echo that sentiment. Jim stood all of five-foot-four or -five, yet he was a towering figure. Bald on top, bright white hair on the sides, a small pot belly that was rock hard. A body that had been shaped and molded by a life of hard work. I mean, who works well into their nineties, as Jim did? You can't teach that type of resilience. The fateful year 2020 finally took my friend, and even after death I find myself continually shaped by his teachings. I've tried to mirror his work ethic and use that passion as an advantage in my life, and doing so has been powerful for me. It's almost like I'm chasing that 80-year-old version of myself.

There are many people trying to navigate life on their own, and I think that path takes much longer. I decided to write this book to inspire others, just as my mentors inspired me. Jim is a man who gave me a series of life lessons until the day he died.

We're all simply travelers on this journey, and I hope to pass along the things I've learned, things that have made a difference in my life, to you.

Life is extremely fragile. It is certainly never guaranteed. If you're like me, you can bank on the struggle part. I call that winner-winner-chicken dinner every time. Bad days can turn into bad weeks that turn into bad months, and before you know it you've had a shitty year. Upon reflection of these types of days, what has been your state of mind? What was your focus? Do you only reflect on the bad?

It's crazy to think about the parallels of the downtrodden— in the moment all we care about is the thing that's bothering us. And it's usually uncontrollable. Fast-forward a few years and look back and you hardly even remember the bad days. Yet I can almost guarantee that you will remember something good that happened then. That is the goal of this book, and the goal for the rest of my life. I want to appreciate the good happening around me right now, today, versus down-the-road during a period of reflection. Perhaps we need to start embracing the darkness in a way that's a little different from ordinary thought.

Having worked for a few years, and getting fairly serious with my girlfriend, we decided that apartment living was no longer a desired path. Money was decent enough. We started looking at small homes and eventually ended up buying this really small house. Nine hundred square feet; that was it. Two bedrooms, bathroom inside the kitchen area, no bigger than a small closet. All that 11 dollars an hour could afford. Luckily, the previous owner had just renovated. I imagine that over the course of a hundred years it had likely seen a few of those renos!

The house was everything we needed, and the timing also felt right to propose to my lady. This girl was truly something. We met shortly after I got home from radio operator training, and we became practically inseparable. We're talking the kind of new love only kids can experience. She became my pen pal during the war, I wore her picture around my neck the whole time, and I often hugged it during what little sleep we got. She gave my life a purpose, something worth fighting for, and I wanted to give her a good life.

But as with many stories, life happens right in front of you—this time in the form of losing my job. No income, and now a new fiancée. I was forced to seek work quickly.

I began working in a factory, third shift, printing dog food bags, and it was god-awful. Showing up to work each night was like a slap in the face. It was the worst. What you do for work is everything. You have to have confidence in who you are, and if you have a job you don't love, it affects your identity. I did that job for four months—it's the only job I've ever walked away from on a whim. I couldn't do it anymore. I was so down on myself; this was not what I wanted for my life. I wanted more. And I knew I was capable of much more and needed to go find it.

This is important to note: I'm not like 95 percent of the males in my family. One could say I broke the mold. I was the first of our family to join the military, the oldest grandson, and first to complete college. These were important goals for me because I had younger siblings and cousins who looked up to me. I wanted to give them a road map to find their way in life. Certainly there have been roadblocks along the way. It took me until my late twenties to graduate from college, but I never gave up. And many to most of those road bumps were due to PTSD and the trauma I experienced in Iraq.

The war in Iraq changed me. I can talk about it now, but for many years I completely internalized everything, and I became so enamored in the silence that it became my life. It hindered my ability; it hindered relationships. I'm only now getting to the point where I'm realizing I can begin the process of healing.

So where did we end up? Out of work, and with responsibilities, I drove my car deep into the big city of Louisville, Kentucky. There are very few jobs outside of factory work where we lived, so I needed to see what the city could offer.

Now the car I drove into Louisville was special in its own right. It cost a thousand bucks, and it came with four tires that went around. That was about all you could say for it. Each time you started the engine, a giant cloud of white smoke billowed from its bowels. My friends used to enjoy that part the best. It lacked power steering and many other finer things—like air conditioning. The heat worked, but it would only blow at max speed, nothing else. One time I got pulled over for speeding. When the trooper approached my window, he said, "The speed limit of this area is 55 miles per hour. Do you know how fast you were going?" I gave my most honest answer: "Yes sir. It registers 80 on the dash, but I can only get her to go 75!" He chuckled as he took my license and registration. There went two hundred dollars and four hours of my life sitting in an online driving school.

At any rate, when I arrived in Louisville I had competing interviews set up, and there was no way I could do both given the distance between them. We didn't have navigation back then to assist with that type of planning. I had directions printed on paper that I got off Mapquest! So I chose the one interview that I thought brought me the best chance of becoming what I wanted. The job description was an entry level sales position. Turns out, this was something I enjoyed during my time selling electronics. Instead, these clowns were selling coupons or something. It was one of those promotional, scam-type deals. Ninety seconds into the conversation it was "thank you for your time," and I slunk back to my car dejected and defeated.

As I sat in that beat-up car, I mustered the courage to call the other company. I just wanted to explain the situation as honestly as I could. Although it was just an entry-level position, I needed the work. Turns out, this business represented one of the largest healthcare companies in America. It was a call center 54 miles, in one direction, from my house, and the position was in their "early out" collections department. I called them, and the lady upfront was Ms. Susan. I told her I had messed up. I believed I had a better opportunity with the other company, I told her honestly, and it hadn't panned out. I said I would love to interview with your company.

As luck would have it, they called me that same day and I was hired on the spot. It was a low-level job that paid eleven dollars an hour. Basically, you show up and sit in an air-conditioned cubicle as the system auto-dials 180 strangers per day. I loved it. I loved communicating and helping others. After about ninety days they asked me to move to another department, one less hectic, one with slightly more earnings potential. And that promotion led to another internal promotion. These promotions were all lateral moves, but after about twelve months I had worked in almost every critical department within the call center. I became well-versed in most areas of operations. The next natural step was to enter a supervisor program.

Usually our lives happen this way, with one step leading to the next, and things never truly planned. If they were planned, perhaps things wouldn't turn out as well as they actually do, but each step on the journey is a little bit of our own mind-set and devices—and a whole lot of divine intervention.

When I was a 15-year-old boy beginning a summer job for the local parks and recreation department, I had no idea what my real currency—not my hourly pay—would be. I found it years later in the form of a lifelong mentor. He started out as a tough boss and worked our crew into the ground. Nonstop, hardly stopping for a break.

That very first summer, in that parks and rec department, was the start of an amazing education about life. There is no way I can put a price on it. Talk about divine intervention. You'll see how valuable of a human being old Jim was.

*"Life is most certainly a heroic journey.
Be strong, and take one day at a time."*

—Jim, my mentor

CHAPTER ONE

From War to the Workplace

Everyone has tackled adversity at some point. I'm no exception. I found the meaning of adversity at a young age. As a teenager I learned to observe the world around me even as I watched my parents struggle. My dad was working, and he was never home. He usually worked twelve-hour shifts. The majority of the week we never saw him. Of course he made decent money, but the money was spent paycheck to paycheck. So we were taken care of, but things were hard for my parents. My dad eventually found a job closer to home. Less hours, probably less pay, and although we saw more of him, it didn't last long. For whatever reason, that position was eliminated.

He and my mother struggled through more adversity after that. Mainly getting a job and trying to keep it. The biggest blow came when we lost our home, and that was a huge issue. The next few years we bounced around living in apartments, rentals, and whatnot. We didn't have much stability. It was a feeling of: *What happens next?*

My parents ended up divorced. A culmination of issues led to that point, all of which happened during my junior year of high school. Old enough to understand what was happening, it was truly devastating for everyone. Oddly enough, my mother became pregnant again during this time. Which meant we're bringing a new member into our family. I'm sixteen years older than this younger sister, and my brother is three years younger than me. Between my sister and I, there was quite an age gap; at times I felt more like a parent that she didn't want or need. But Janea also became a sort of fresh start for everyone. This tiny human garnered just the right amount of attention. I was also fully aware of the financial hardships of divorce, separate living arrangements, and now three kids. I had no choice but to work. I wanted to help my family.

Work has always been an outlet. One thing that always stuck with me, from my time with Jim, my mentor later in life, was this statement (Jim had tons of wisdom): "When things are going wrong at home, or they're going wrong with your significant other, just go and take it out on your work. Go to work!" That's where you check everything bothering you at the door and focus on completing your tasks. Oh, by the way, you're also earning a little bit of money while doing so. Now money isn't going to fix anything, nor will it solve all your problems, but it's going to help you more than it hurts you. I've been around wealthy people in my life. I've even made decent money, but doing so doesn't make the problems of everyday life disappear. Earning money creates opportunities. So choose to work so you can afford to live. That's a powerful thought.

During this period of early work and trying to do my part, I had an eye-opening experience. One snowy evening in the middle of winter, I had just gotten off a late night shift at Arby's. My mother was sleeping on a couch with my sister, who wasn't feeling well. Where we were living it was my mother, my sister, my brother, and myself; however, after the divorce, my brother also spent a lot of time with our grandparents. He wasn't home that night, so it was just my mom, my sister, and me. We lived in a bad area of town, but it was a place my mom could afford. Across the street was an apartment complex, and some of those tenants were less than desirable neighbors. Anyway, one of those individuals decided they were going to try to kick in our front door in the middle of the night.

I remember being awakened by my mom, panicked, who said, "Josh, grab your brother's gun."

Rushing into my brother's room, I grabbed his shotgun off the wall. That's the first time I ever pointed my weapon at another human being. As this intruder kept kicking on the door, I racked a round into the chamber. The sound must have carried louder than the obscenities I had been yelling at him. It's funny to think about now. What stands out isn't the guy trying to make entry, and it isn't the fact that I quite possibly would have had to engage him with a weapon. It was the fact that my mom yelled for me to grab my younger brother's gun. As the oldest, I was supposed to be the toughest, right? I mean, there was a period in my life where I probably did get the best of my brother.

But truth be told, all of that big brother attention given to me actually gave him an incredible edge. He may not know it, but he will always be much tougher than me. Why? His path was the opposite of mine: he often took on life in a way that was much harder for him. There's this: he met a girl early on and became infatuated. They ended up living together during high school as he lived with our grandparents. That type of arrangement really forced two children to grow up early. All my brother has ever known is working in a factory as a manual laborer, a job that he is very thankful for—but he works really hard to provide for his family. I admire this about my brother: his ability to live. What I mean by that is, from the outside looking in, some decisions he makes may seem sporadic, but he finds enjoyment and fulfillment in things he enjoys. He loves the outdoors.

Jake, my younger brother, is a remarkable outdoorsman like most of the males in my family. They can hunt, fish, and trap. Their entire life is consumed by the outdoors. It's odd sometimes trying to connect with your family members during the holidays. They're all talking about their hunt, their deer stands, their whatever—here I am with nothing to say. It wasn't until I joined the Marines and started hunting *people* that I began to obtain the rights to my "man card" at the kitchen table.

So there I was, a teenager, the outcast, grabbing the gun off my brother's wall.

Growing up, I remember going on hunting trips and my grandfather trying to get me involved. Often I would just fall asleep in the truck as he chased down his hounds in the middle of the night. So, hearing "grab your brother's gun" is memorable because I probably should have gone to get my own, but I didn't have one! This is just one example of having to act fast in the moment. I had to learn this, and it would become a huge theme in my life.

On New Year's Day 2018 I was coming off a great yet low-key night with my best friend and his family. We have boys similar in age, so things didn't get too wild. The morning after, around 9 AM, the phone rang. It was my mother . . .

Part of my journey in arriving at this book came from the motivation of my peers. I was afforded the opportunity to meet Marcus Luttrell, author of *Lone Survivor*. Marcus is an American hero, and in no way, shape, or form did I or will I live up to what he endured. But it was at a private meet-and-greet that we shared a brief conversation. When Marcus arrived, the crowd was fixated. He migrated to my corner; that seemed to be a safe place. After a few book signings, someone said, "Hey Marcus, get a picture with my Marine friend."

His focus quickly shifted, and we began to talk about our time in Iraq. Turns out he was there during the invasion as well. He had glowing things to say about the Marines and turned to the audience and said, "These guys right here did heroic things over there and should be celebrated."

Talk about validating. My industry peers knew I served, but this truly brought things full circle.

A few months later over dinner, a good buddy, Jon Levine, said to me, "Why don't you speak on your life's experiences? I got a little event coming up that I am curating, and I'm booking you for this event. You need to share your story." True to his word, he booked me. Talk about being out of your comfort zone! Speaking of some of these stories, some of these trials and tribulations, was new for me. I was used to internalizing everything, living privately.

During this presentation, I spoke about that night a couple of years earlier, referring to it as "Chaos Whispers." That morning my mother called me . . .

Out of breath, frantic, she whispered my name three times. "Joshua . . . Joshua . . . Joshua."

I thought maybe it had to do with my dad; he had suffered a stroke that year and wasn't in the best of health.

She frantically explained, "They found your cousin Morgan dead. They found the body on the side of the road out past your grandparents' house."

All I could do was rush out there. This particular morning was brutal, the temperatures well below zero factoring in the wind chill. This is a place where my grandparents lived, and it served as the hub of my childhood. Our home was built just above theirs on the hill, and we all lived and grew up playing in this area. It was special to us. We dubbed the area Wonderland. My grandparents purchased this land back in the mid-eighties. It was on several acres of wooded area that had been cleared off. There were only a few homes toward the end of that road; it turned into an old gravel road in the middle of nowheresville, Indiana. We grew up pretty much in the sticks next to this nature preserve.

For much of my life, I could remember nothing but happiness with that particular area. This day, however, an older couple driving by found my younger cousin there. Her body was frozen and lifeless, thrown out there on the side of the gravel road like a piece of trash. It was truly heartbreaking. The last person who saw her alive was a boyfriend. As I rushed up to be with my family, there were news choppers flying overhead, state police and sheriff's deputies working the scene, and I was trying to make some sense of it all.

Under a blanket, I saw my cousin's body. By the time I entered my grandfather's house, I was greeted with gut-wrenching cries and sorrow—including from Morgan's brother, who I cherish as my own brother. All we could do was try to console one another. The atmosphere was unreal. Nobody could believe it happened. I sat at the kitchen table with my grandfather. For whatever reason, the sheriff's deputy had asked him to ID the body.

My grandfather, 78 and coming off one of his hardest years after burying his wife a few months back, sat quietly. That's the last thing he needed to see: a dead grandchild, someone who had been living with him. His eyes and face were somehow familiar, like he had seen the great beyond. I've seen that type of trauma before, that kind of shock and awe. You see, a person gets a sort of thousand-yard stare. As we sat there, my grandfather and I talked through one of the most real conversations we ever had—about what he saw and how it made him feel. Never in our thirty-five years together had we shared a moment so deep. I could tell he was shook, rocked to his core. I could relate to him—for once.

"We need to call Robin," my mom said, referring to Morgan's mother.

An hour had gone by, and Robin still didn't know. Robin and my uncle had divorced more than ten years earlier, and she was living in Kansas City working as a flight attendant, so she wasn't in the area (and could be anywhere, for that matter). A few of my family tried to reach out through Facebook Messenger with no immediate connection. For whatever reason, and simply because I was deemed one of the strongest in the room, the pressure was on me. "You need to try and make this call," someone said.

The first time I dialed, no answer. *Thank God,* I thought. I literally had to go outside and try to collect my thoughts, try to figure out the proper way of telling a mother that her daughter was dead. Someone else said: "Josh, you're built for this. You can do this. You're tough. Just make the damn call."

When I tell you I was not prepared or qualified to make that call, I am telling you I was not prepared for the unprecedented hurt and pain that came through the other end of that line when we were finally able to connect. *That* very moment. Forget anything I had ever done—this moment broke my spirit . . .

. . . . I had a little more confidence in life at that point. I had just closed the largest deal in my company's history, by far, just three weeks earlier. It was an impressive feat that was sort of a culmination of hard work and perseverance. A huge upswing for the business. So I knew inside that I could be a strong voice when trying to comfort Robin. But business, of course, is different from family. After I made that call, the impact was bigger than anything I had expected. I was in a bad spot mentally. Everything that had been in the back of my mind from my experiences in the war—all of that pain came rushing back. I had no clue *this* would be a turning point in my life. I don't even remember the words exchanged with Robin, but I remember the screams that came out on the receiving end. They were loud, haunting, nightmarish.

Traumatic experiences need time to process; time does work to cauterize the damage and begin to numb the pain. This I do know. What I haven't found out how to overcome is dealing with the moments immediately after; I wasn't in a good place mentally after these events.

I ended up quitting my job—even after I had closed that all-time record deal. I don't know why I did it; in retrospect, it was very dumb. But I felt like a change was needed. What I really should have asked for was a couple of weeks. My leadership would have obliged.

Thankfully, eight months later they invited me back—and this is a true testament to being valued. I will never forget that olive branch. While away I actually grew up a bit more professionally.

I was living out of my comfort zone, meeting new faces, and I made a good friend along the way. Justin was several years younger than me, but he was brilliant and completely undervalued. I saw a lot of potential in him and wanted to inspire him, help him succeed. Sometimes all a person needs is self-assurance; the kids these days call that gassing someone up. Justin didn't need me; he needed gas and someone to get out of his way. I just helped provide that.

Morgan's death changed me immensely; facing her death was probably the most adverse thing I'd ever gone through. Seeing my family in such a fragile state, a family member thrown out like a piece of trash, was the definition of messed up. Losing a child, a sibling, relative—anyone you care about—I don't wish that kind of death on anyone. To be honest, it is awkward even to this day to talk about.

Everyone gets lost in their environment at times. It's hard to navigate outside of what we're born into or what career we choose first. Naturally, life in the military is another example of adversity. You're expected to get through many objectives quickly and efficiently. Being in the Marines defined everything for me. "They're tough," people say. That pressure catalyzed me, in a way, and prepared me for this crazy life and the family I was born into.

After high school I tried to join a buddy program. The goal was to leave about six days after high school graduation; the problem was my age. At 17, it would require my parents' approval to sign up. There was no shot my parents would sign off on this.

It was early 2001, and my mom told me, "You'll end up getting your ass sent off to war."

I tried to soothe her concern. "We're not going to war, Mom. When was the last time that happened?" And my dad? He just wanted me to go to work; he didn't get the whole military vibe.

I wanted to enter so badly. I didn't have many answers. I just knew I needed to do something law enforcement-related or something federal like a US Marshal. In order to get to that federal level, having military experience would help. During high school career days, there was a position to shadow a state police officer that my mother knew from my sister's daycare. It was an epic ride-along: not only was it the day after a hostage situation that turned homicide, there was also a suicide. Most of the day was dealing with death, being shown pictures. This guy used the opportunity to see if I had the guts to withstand the wickedness of the world. I never averted my eyes. It was inside of me; I could handle the job.

So this became my plan: head to college and study criminal justice. Two weeks into my first year of college I am sitting in a computer lab with my friends, illegally downloading songs from the Internet and trying to burn them to a CD. And then it happened . . .

. . . It was all over the Internet and TV monitors. Students gathered en masse and watched two planes—aircraft full of Americans—fly into the World Trade Center. At that moment all I could think about was two friends I should have been in boot camp with. Both were set to come home a few weeks later. When one of them did, James and I spent some time together; he was a longtime friend who shared his love of the Marines. So, in reality, he was motivated more than ever by those events. That's when I knew my life was going to change. I was going to be a Marine.

James and I went down to the local recruiter's office and made it happen. Then I had to break it to my mom. So, of course, the very next day she marched her little curly-headed self down to that recruiter's office and let him have the business. Gunny Murphy was built like a Greek god, a six-foot-four tattooed brute of a human being. "Mrs. White . . . Mrs. White . . . " He was just trying to edge a word in. To his credit, he managed to get my mom talking about her concerns and offered a compromise. "Your son can still serve as a Marine and finish his college education as a reservist."

As with anyone who joins the military, once you get that burning desire, it cannot be extinguished. An 18-year-old man—really, a young kid—I was angry at what I saw. September 11, 2001 was my motivation to serve my country. *This is it,* I told myself. So on November 26, 2001, I flew across the country, arriving at midnight at Marine Corps Recruit Depot (MCRD), San Diego, California. This was home to the Hollywood Marines!

For the next few months, the last words that come out of my mouth were "Yes, sir!" or "No, sir!" From the moment we stepped off that bus they broke us down so they could build us back up—physically and mentally. The "lean, mean fighting machine" cliché is no joke. That's when I knew I was built for something a little bit more than the game hunting the men in my family loved.

* * * * *

Fast-forward to January 2003, after boot camp, combat training, and my military occupational training (radio operator). I was challenged yet again. One of the compromises made with my mom was going to school while serving. She always wanted me to have an education, and I wanted to do that for her. I know they tell you to listen to your mother—how she knew was beyond me—and her biggest fear was seeing me go off to fight a war. Listen to your parents, folks; they are rarely wrong. Indeed, one day I would be called up to fight a war.

A few months after transitioning back and settling into the reserve way of life, we got fitted for the new digital cammies the Marines were rolling out. This was October 2002 and it was over one drill weekend. Everyone was speculating on why they would be issuing us desert formats. For December's drill we received news that we would be getting an anthrax vaccine. This would require a booster a couple of weeks after the initial shot. Meaning we would have to return on an off-drill weekend to receive the booster.

Nothing elaborate; a quick trip up to the naval armory in Indianapolis to get a shot and then come home. So on a very cold January day we showed up for that booster. All of our company brass were there, and they called everyone to attention to read this statement:

As of 12:01 last night Det Comm
Company has been mobilized for Operation
Enduring Freedom. You have seventy-two
hours to get your affairs in order.

We were shocked. *Where would we be going? Seventy-two hours? That's not a lot of time for affairs! I'm 19! What kind of affairs do I have?*

What it really meant was "talk to your family" and "begin writing your will." Prepare yourselves to fight. The only problem: nobody knew where we were going to fight. This created a lot of awkward goodbye situations. My family and girlfriend were completely distraught. I have some amazing friends. From the moments leading up to when I joined and throughout (many sent me letters), to picking me up from the airport to surprise my family, to throwing parties, my friends were there to support me. It was very awkward for everyone to say goodbye, because who really thought that, even still, there would be a war? They only knew I was going somewhere high-risk. There were talks, at that point, of Iraq, but we didn't know until the middle of February where we were headed. In the end, we were headed to Kuwait in support of the 1st Marine Division. My mother, grandmother, and girlfriend drove all night to the base in Camp LeJuene once they knew I had a departure date. They wanted to see me one last time.

Then we hopped on a commercial flight, weapons and all, and flew overnight (a very long flight), stopping in places like Frankfurt, Germany, before making our way to Kuwait. We arrived under cover of darkness and quickly went through some receiving type of check-in procedures before boarding a bus and being shuttled to the middle of nowhere in the middle of the desert. This area became known as Camp Matilda. We would help build this psuedo tent city.

Just weeks prior I had been in a comfortable place, a teenager sitting around playing Xbox with buddies. What a difference a few weeks can make. I now found myself literally on the border of Iraq/Kuwait with the 1st Marine Division, and in a few weeks we would be crossing the line of departure and invading a country. Everything was becoming more and more surreal.

I remember General Mattis providing us a letter and delivering a motivational speech about the fight that lay ahead. He talked about how difficult this journey would be, but that we should never get discouraged. He asked us to look to the left and right and never worry about having enough support. We had brought enough firepower, he said. It was the most goosebump-driven speech I have ever experienced, and that type of energy and confidence is intoxicating. You literally feel unstoppable. While not as intense, the type of confidence gained from those experiences would end up helping me within the civilian workforce.

* * * * *

In that workforce: I started out in an entry-level job and worked my way up to supervisor-manager. Then I ended up having the wherewithal to apply for a position that I wasn't qualified for—along with many more qualified candidates who had been senior managers for the company a lot longer than I had been there. This became another example of how I would overcome circumstances and push forward to my desired outcome.

At the time, I was a 26-year-old kid who hadn't quite finished college yet. The only thing I had going for me was my work ethic and the fact I could draw from experiences in the Marines. The interviews were grueling. Usually in group format, with management level personnel or executives taking part in the roundtable. The questions were to be answered in a particular format, in which you had to explain the situation or task, explain your actions, and the root cause or result of those actions. During the interview process, I was asked, "Josh, tell me about a time in your life when you were stressed."

I don't remember the exact story shared, but I do remember leaning back in my chair a bit and getting this little smile on my face prior to sharing. I didn't really have a stressful, cookie-cutter-type story from my time served at this company, and that is likely how my competitors answered. I chose to go rogue and share some stressful moments experienced during my time in the war zone. You could have heard a pin drop. Who would have thought something like that would have translated to the business setting? My service became a tremendous value-add that provided an advantage for a position I wasn't quite ready for on paper. Though I knew I was ready for it, I just had to share enough about myself to gain their trust and give me the opportunity. That's when I started looking at the war much differently, turning those struggles into positives, applying those abilities gained in tough situations, and those would eventually help gain a supervisor role and a position to lead others. The promotions kept coming until I was in a role that was client-facing, which meant I would be serving as a direct liaison between our business and those we serve.

For perspective, how many young adults do you know who have had experience in highly stressful areas and displayed the ability to make decisions and thrive? I learned to adapt to mold myself into that role, not only from a professional standpoint but also a personal one. I took a lot of pride in being that person for my family and knowing that I'm stable. Not perfect, but functional.

It's a common thing we laugh about in our home. We say, "Nobody ever worries about us." Or people have said, "We don't worry about you. We know you take care of your kids. You're going to be (this) or (that)."

These are nice affirmations, but there is another truth. If they only knew the internal struggles I have dealing with my PTSD and hypervigilance—which, by the way, is extremely exhausting and overwhelming at times. If they only knew I'm not completely "strong" or confident in my abilities all the time, they would understand there is a human on the other side of this, one who gets triggered easily and truly has to work on himself. (Then, perhaps, they would choose their words more carefully.) But this is mostly my fault. I do not verbalize to anyone. I keep my feelings, my emotions, to myself. Often when family members do get something out of me, it comes across as short or disinterested. I hate that about myself.

I'm grateful for my life now, but most days aren't easy. We can all relate to that. Sometimes I'm not the easiest person to get along with, or I'm constantly thinking about things normal people don't think about or worry about. The hypervigilance is something I cannot turn off; I am constantly in a state of observation. Planning or speculating, in my mind, the "next big thing" for myself or my family—this is a huge distraction from the overall ability to feel. Feelings in general—instead of numbness—would actually be welcomed!

My life's experiences have proved it doesn't matter what you achieve. The strongest of people can face that pain head-on instead of denying or buying it off. I experienced so much suffering through the last few years watching family members pass, the shock of Morgan's death, and my father's health deteriorating. These deaths were extremely close to home, a once "happy place" for my family where I would gather. So many fond memories have been replaced these past few years with these images of death and sadness.

I love my family, but we are as dysfunctional as you can get. You do not get to choose your family, and in no way, shape, or form would I replace any of them. I love them all unconditionally. If I had the power to change the path or the decisions of some, absolutely, I would. But that is not feasible. All I can do is acknowledge what is there and do my best to lead this next generation away from the pain and sorrow, the poverty. I used to be ashamed of certain things, but that changed when I learned to accept the human, the person I loved, and not approve of their actions. You can love someone, but you don't have to love how they are or how they treat others. Some of my favorite people on earth are addicts; they're sick. I cannot change that. But when I see them, on occasion, I can show them my love. That's all I have to give. My goals are focused not on the selfish behavior of the few, but on the long-term well-being of their future. I keep reminding myself the future belongs to my kids.

Despite our struggles, I love my family and want to help them take steps forward to the point that future generations don't have to deal with so much pain. I want to be the one who carries us into the next generation and doesn't have to carry pain, hear about it, speak it, or live through it.

So I often find myself asking this question: How can I transition and transform those around me?

Everyone's looking at me as this beacon of hope, but now I've got to give them a look at the real me, the one who has been transformed through experiences and pain. We have to hurt to heal, as they say, and we have to verbalize our trauma. Learn how to become an effective medium to express that, to communicate. (I'm not a verbal person when it comes to adversity or pain, so writing a book was my best outlet.) I want my family to know this: "Don't worry. I have your back." But also: "This is who I am"—that is, a work in progress.

Nobody wants to come off as weak and vulnerable. Play that role in the military and you're the first one out. Play that role in life—when it comes to family and relationships—and you might let others down. This is how I perceive the world. Having so many people look up to you or turn to you for guidance, placing their trust in you, and you've given them every reason to believe they can give that trust. Rising to the occasion, time after time, is how they see you. However, you know there are chinks in the armor. For me, choosing to speak with a therapist and seek care—this has been eye-opening. Hearing you have post-traumatic stress disorder doesn't remove the weight, it just gives you peace of mind. It's like you finally understand: there is a reason I act this way. Why do I feel this way? Why I choose to hold things in, and why I cannot feel . . . much of anything.

Think about something you love to do, something crazy that gives you the most intense rush of adrenaline. I haven't experienced much of anything that can match the adrenaline dump experienced in Iraq. Maybe I need to go jump out of a plane or something crazy like that.

When you think you need help? Trust me, don't wait. It took me seventeen years to talk to someone about my experiences and how they affected me as a young adult and as a man today. I wasn't always "right" about my decisions back then—and I don't know how I got to the place I am now other than hard work—but all we can do is acknowledge, appreciate, and learn the lessons. At times, it's okay not to be okay. For a lot of mental weight I deal with, just because nobody worries or thinks to ask, I internalize my pain. I replay the chaos in my mind often, and there has been this sort of safety within the silence. Sometimes, that's what the aftermath of suffering is: chaos, swirling, destruction.

Next time, think of your tragedy and pain like a storm. It is a natural occurrence, and the memories will pop up from time to time. Dealing with your internal storm—acknowledging its place within you—is better than letting it tear you apart. Every day I have triggers, but for the most part I keep them in. Silence becomes safe. I've had to learn through these events, these experiences in my life, that maybe I'm not as strong as I thought, that my security blanket of silence no longer has the ability to coexist, and I chose to seek help. I'm glad I did. Sometimes we can't contextualize certain kinds of trauma until years later—especially when they're war-related.

* * * * *

In Iraq we were constantly on the move. Clearing buildings, areas, locals who were threats. All the while maneuvering in the Humvee. You know all about the perceived threat, and then you have to execute the mission. A coalition force invaded a country with known threats. We were expecting to be hit with ground troops, artillery, radicals, tanks, and chemical weapons. This was an actual war.

Factor in that we are in the middle of the desert—it gets hot! We are in woodland-scheme chemical suits with a combat load. Hot. *Hot.* There was a point where I didn't shower for sixty days! And once we were in, we were in the thick of it. We drove in a convoy all the way to Baghdad. It was a "move or die" mentality. You go through heightened senses with combat going on all around you for months—and then you come home. You get dropped back off in the civilian world. It's like the Fourth of July with firecrackers going off. I'm hitting the deck, and I don't know what's going on. I start to have these wild dreams, and I try to process what I just experienced, all the while trying to lead a normal life. You cannot lead a normal life after that. There has to be a level of acceptance of a new norm.

At the time, I didn't have a career path. Remember, the goal was Marines plus College = Career in Law Enforcement. I wanted to move out and go to college, live with my friends. Meanwhile, most of them are trying to be normal, knuckle-headed 21-year-olds. I was just different and couldn't relate. College was not working out. I would avoid it and return to my room, try to sleep the day away. Class was difficult because I couldn't turn off the awareness of others. Their movements, the loud noises of slamming books on the desk, all of this startled me. There were other irritants; it was hard to focus. I discovered it best to show up early to classes so I could migrate to the corner in the back; that way I could at least feel most comfortable.

Work, at that point, was the only outlet I had. Nervous and edgy, it didn't feel right being in class at school. Anxiety attacks became regular, like some damn heart attack. Shortly after I just quit going to school and focused on my isolation and work.

When you're back in the real world, you don't have your Marines to your left and right. I didn't know how to process being a regular person anymore. Being stationed overseas, in the midst of a war, was so life-altering that I was numb to emotion. It wasn't until my wife—the same girlfriend who saw me before I shipped off; we ended up married—and I welcomed our first child in 2012 that I felt something again. Almost nine years after returning home it became harder to feel. I was numb, callous, heartless . . . until I laid eyes on my son. It was such an overwhelming experience.

When they handed him to me, I broke down. It wasn't just a good cry. It was one of those ugly cries, one I couldn't control or stop. It just had to work its way out. What was this feeling? It had been so long. I didn't cry when my cousin Morgan died. That angered me in a tragic kind of way, which is a weird thing to say. Back then, I was in fight mode. Grief hits all of us differently. I shared a moment with my grandmother on her deathbed. She had become nonverbal from the brain damage, but her eyes let me know she understood this would be the final time we saw one another on this earth. I felt the gravity of that goodbye. When my grandfather passed away, coincidently on my birthday, it was different. It wasn't really a cry; rather, again, it was this goodbye of sorts. He wasn't an educated man. He was very simple and lived extremely poor his final years. He gave all he could for those who needed him. He left me with a final departing message of hope. While lying there, on oxygen, he asked me for some water. As I swabbed his mouth, he looked over at my mother and said, "I'm ready."

"What?" she asked.

"I miss talking about her . . . " He trailed off in thought, referring to his wife, my grandma.

"I know you do," she said. "I know you're ready."

"I love her. I miss her. I just want to be with her."

Right there, that statement—I felt that. Another time, when I walked in the door and got ready to go to Iraq, I saw my dad cry. There were a lot of emotions and feelings before shipping off to war. There wasn't a dry eye at the naval building when we were sent away. In fact, it was the first time my family saw me with a rifle slung over my shoulder. The *Indianapolis Star* captured a photo of my dad and I sharing a moment. My Marines loved that; there was plenty of time for them to heckle.

The scene: families saying goodbye. My dad, he was something else. Upon returning from the 72-hour check-in he walked me to the door to check back in. We got to the steps and he couldn't control himself. For me, it was one of the first times seeing that man actually cry. There is something about seeing your heroes, the ones you look up to, in such a vulnerable state.

So, back to when my son was born: knowing I would be responsible for this small child's life, I saw myself reborn without any of the flaws or any of the damage—a clean slate. These are the times when we cling to what is pure and good and what matters in life. When my grandfather expressed his desire to be with my grandmother, you understood the power of that statement and what she meant to him.

Having our reasons, our purpose for why we fight, is what we thrive on as warriors. When you're in the thick of it, you have to focus on the things that will keep you alive as much as the things that will kill you. Regardless of where you're at, especially in combat, you never want to let your brother down. That's all an act of intimacy, 100 percent. It's not about you anymore. It's about not letting the person beside you down.

Your heart grows, and it's bigger than the space you're standing in.

Death is death. Death, however, has taught me so many things. Everyone dies, and boy, would it be nice to know the expiration date. But if you could know, would you want to? Death is a valuable teacher; there is no lesson more glaring than gaining an overall appreciation for life. There is something to be said about tiptoeing the line of death, about truly finding out who you are, what you are made of, and valuing the opportunity of the day. I can assure you, those who have paid the ultimate sacrifice, or who have lost their battle, would have found a way to appreciate the day. We cannot let those sacrifices go to waste; we are free because of them.

A question plenty of folks have asked: do you miss it? Of course you miss it. You have to define what you miss, though. It all comes down to what you were willing to put in, where you saw yourself, and if those goals lined up. The military has helped me, and it has hurt me. But the best part, after all the pain and sacrifice: you miss the people. It always comes down to people. I am not talking about the interaction you get from browsing a social media profile. That human-to-human connection, or bond—that is what I miss most about my brothers.

When you spend eight hours a day handling healthcare and finance-related topics, there aren't a lot of adrenaline-inducing scenarios. Although it wasn't the career path I saw for myself, I love it. I belong here, and I am most thankful for it. Adrenaline is the addiction of doing the "crazy stuff" in service, and it left me wanting to find it again.

So I joined a local volunteer fire service in my hometown, and I loved being there. From the camaraderie of the guys, to kicking in the door, to going into a burning building after

43

arriving at the scene of a fire, I found myself serving again. It felt good. (I don't think people appreciate the fire service like they should. Outside of big cities, most of these towns are supported by volunteers who are willing to put their life on the line to protect lives and property.)

Chasing the extreme just to feel adrenaline is not for normal folks. Although I yearn for it, there isn't anything that doesn't involve extreme risk that I have found that matches the high you get. Adrenaline, fear, the imminent threat of danger: these were the things we ran on over there, in Iraq, and we very well could have died.

So running around chasing housefires filled a need. But firefighters are also exposed to some of the things I don't miss anymore. I wasn't ready for a game with death again. I am not talking about natural death; we can all learn to cope with natural passing. It's the tragic deaths, caused from accidents, explosions, gunfire, or wickedness. Have you ever smelled a rotting corpse? Have you ever picked up body parts from a human being or rushed to the aid of someone trapped who eventually was consumed by the event? What about younger kids who drive too fast and wrap themselves around a tree, and they have to be cut out. That fear, that pain—all of that blended together with the events that shocked me in my teens. I did not get adrenaline from those moments. It would put me in an all too familiar place I wanted to forget. Now, there are some people who are going to read this and call me soft. "Suck it up; you signed up for this. I do this for a living each and every day, and it doesn't bother me." My answer: Great. We need strong-willed people to handle those types of things. But what they probably haven't experienced yet is their moment, their limit where it affects their day-to-day; maybe they are just in denial or completely numb or calloused. Everyone is different: our minds, our bodies, our souls. These are unique to ourselves, and these are why, unless we are willing to walk a few steps in another person's shoes, we shouldn't pass judgement.

Once I saw the aftermath of an EF-4 Tornado. We were one of the first neighboring counties to arrive on scene. It was something straight out of the movie *Twister*. I had seen destruction before: buildings toppled, cars exploded. But I had never seen such sheer power of mother nature. She hurled school buses from a parking lot to a building across the street. She stripped houses down to their foundations. The local elementary school had been leveled, along with all the homes in its path. Thankfully, the leadership made the right call that day and everyone had evacuated the school. However, we cleared the school making sure no one—God forbid, any kids—were trapped. Imagine a bomb going off, sending devastation and debris everywhere. It looked like that.

I realize my life could have gone a few different ways after Iraq. I could have turned to the bottle or drugs. I had access to all of that. I chose work, and not just the kind that pays you. I chose to read, to learn from trial and error. This works, but it also doesn't (for me). I didn't want to burden my parents, so I worked. My goals were still the same: change the history that has plagued our family; break that cycle of struggle and pain. You have to find a new fight, something that drives you. I am afraid of letting down the folks who depend on me, disappointing them.

What fuels you? What do you need to gain from this moment? What do you need to pay more attention to, or give yourself credit for, right now? Surely there is something. Maybe it's just granular, like you got out of bed today and made your bed. (An aside, but I find this important: I cannot tell you how satisfying it is to wake up and make your bed. It's starting off the day by accomplishing one simple task. The most benefit I get from that task is arriving back to that same bed later that night and crawling into the sheets of a made bed; it just feels better. Give yourself that luxury every day. Then you can move to the next achievement.)

Sometimes these moments come out of nowhere. The guy I sat with in the computer lab when the towers fell, his name was Dustin Jones. Dustin's girlfriend's family made good money. They owned a giant house on top of this rolling hill in one of the nicer neighborhoods of town. Dustin and I had been childhood friends since elementary school. We were fierce adversaries on the basketball court in those days, but Dustin was nonetheless a friend we all admired. His laugh would reel you in; you wanted to be around someone like him. He had big aspirations and wanted to become an optometrist.

Tragically, Dustin passed before reaching his dream; he died in a car accident. I looked up to him, as do most of my close friends. These friends are dreamers; they chase down their goals. It's exciting to see them obtain their goals and become leaders and good parents. It's important who you invite into your circle, as those folks play a heavy influence on your day-to-day outlook. You learn from them; it becomes a sort of motivation to do better yourself. The wrong friends and the wrong energy will take you down, which is why I appreciate my friends more than they could ever know.

One of my strongest memories of Dustin was picking him up one night over at his girl's house. Before stepping out he needed to take an Advil or something. I remember him drinking some water and reaching over to grab some paper towels.

A bit humorously, he grabbed an egregious amount of towels to wipe his mouth. The fact he grabbed so many paper towels, so frivolously, stuck out to me. We never had paper towels at my house, and if we did, you didn't use them to wipe your mouth! My momma used them for cleaning. So I stood there, amazed at what life had handed my friend. I laugh to myself when I tell this story, because it's just paper towels—but it means something to me.

A couple months ago I'm sitting and watching my seven-year-old. He walks over and grabs something to drink, and in the process, without hesitation—just like Dustin—grabs an enormous amount of paper towels to wipe his mouth. I thought about my friend at that moment. It made me happy. It was like that subtle nod from a friend, like, "You made it, my friend. You are now that type of provider for your son."

As long as I'm breathing, I'll fight so my son doesn't have to experience the deepest struggles. Of course, there will come a time when he will have to learn to work and become a man, but my goal is to continue building him up so he doesn't have to overcome the same level of pain and adversity. I want a simple, normal life for him. That's my fight. That's my journey.

If you haven't found yours, look closer. There's a reason to live, to fight. Maybe you're just overlooking it.

CHAPTER TWO

Heroes

Who were your early heroes? For some, the answer is no one, and if that's true for you I want you to make the decision today to be your own hero—and realize you're not alone. You meet so many people in your life, and choosing the right ones to pour into you and guide you is important.

I can't write my story without mentioning those who shaped me along the way. It's important to share a little bit of the history of my parents. I had a solid foundation and support system.

I grew up in a small town in Southern Indiana, a little farm community. It was like any little Midwestern town during the time, one occupied by working middle-class people. Folks back then took pride, there were decent jobs, and we rallied around our local sports teams.

My brother and I grew up with the love of basketball, which was passed down from our father. My dad was obsessed with basketball, always playing or watching it. But my dad played basketball differently. His passion derived from his experiences.

He is a survivor. When he was younger, his mother gave him up. She ran off with a circus carny. (This thought came to mind as I wrote that last line: what a dumb thing to say out loud—or, even, to write.) All three of her youngest—and she had at least seven to eight kids—entered the system. My dad shared about staying at this group home for about three years—until he ran away. He bounced in and out of foster care.

Where was his dad? He was just an old drunk, unreliable. What type of person just gives their children up? That has to create a very lonely childhood.

My dad talked about bouncing around from home to home, and he was in more than ten. He spoke about this one family. When he would come home from school, the only thing he could get for dinner was cold cheese sandwiches, and he would have to eat away from everybody else in the family. In the garage. This was the ultimate rejection. And this after being rejected by his biological mother.

Looking back, I see how my father's adversity was actually the cornerstone for who he became. If he could survive the hurt at such an early age, can't we overcome adversity?

The family I grew up in always seemed to be caught in a cyclical stage of adversity. It's almost like a New Year's resolution: new attempts to start over, again and again. What kind of messed-up things can we avoid this year?

Despite the trials and tribulations from being given away and everything that came with that, my dad did not display any bitterness toward his mother. In fact, when we were old enough, he brought us to visit her.

My father dealt with his pain differently. Despite being surrounded by alcoholics, he has never drank so much as an ounce of alcohol—all out of fear of what he would become. His entire life he has frowned upon any type of drinking, a true example of strength and willpower.

Honor. You can learn a lot about honor and truth from your mentors, yet even more from those who raised you—or those who didn't.

My father's mother was wheelchair-bound after she had an accident. It was purgatory for her, sitting around in a wheelchair, surrounded by adult kids who struggled with addiction. Most of them died at young ages. She died when I was in Iraq. My father didn't want to bother me with the news of her passing until I got home. He wanted me to focus on returning home. Not that I would have shed a tear. As a parent myself, I am ashamed for her. Circus. A life right out of a circus.

My mother experienced a different type of upbringing. She was the second of four children, the only daughter. Her father, Willie, was a carpenter, an avid lover of the outdoors. My mom talked about all the outdoor adventures the children would go on with their parents. She loved her youth, and I enjoy when she shares those stories.

After I graduated, the little hometown I grew up in was hit with too many drugs. It wasn't quite the nice little middle-class town I grew up in. It became infused with drugs. Too many friends and family members were impacted by drugs. There was too much despair.

When I was with the fire department, I heard radio traffic about a stabbing that happened out in the area where I grew up. It turned out to be my mother's youngest two brothers. Sadly, they were always fighting and up to no good. This time was different. One meth-laden uncle decided to carve up the other and leave him for dead. It was a traumatic thing for my grandparents to see. My grandmother died inside that day—and, not too long after it, physically. When drugs enter your family, they eat away at the very core of its existence.

I went from this wonderful upbringing . . . to viewing how drugs can literally destroy everything.

I'm grateful my parents turned out differently. Their burdens did not become hereditary.

I'm not saying that all my relatives are poor human beings, but you have to paint a picture of reality the way it really is: some people within my family are not great people. They're not productive members of society. They are selfish and destroy anything in their path. My grandparents were probably too soft regarding some of them, and I don't blame them for that. They did what they thought was best, but it also cost them dearly. They died with so very little. They couldn't even enjoy their twilight years.

So I made a decision to uproot that family tree. I figured that's the only hope for the next generation. Those are lessons learned from and mixed with my grandparents' strife. If you don't raise your kids, you will end up raising your grandkids, and all the mess that comes between.

My mom has always been caught in the middle. Forget the BS brought on by her younger brothers. My mom had to endure a relationship with her mom that wasn't what you would think it would be for an only daughter. My grandmother was so hard on my mother, and it was difficult for her. Instead of being this only daughter and having a close relationship with her mom, well, it never happened. My grandmother was unbelievably tough. She was one of the toughest people I ever met: a scarred-up body, fearless. Relationships are complex sometimes, especially with family.

I didn't know about all the dysfunction until I got older. That soured my relationship with my grandmother in the later years because I tried to take a stand against that behavior on my mother's behalf. Here she was working third shift—mind you, working, unlike her brothers—and she couldn't get any help or support. Instead she was given tough rhetoric about having kids at her age. It was all dysfunctional to say the least, but that didn't stop my mother from loving her mom. Despite being pushed away and talked down to, she never faltered in her love. My grandmother did know how to love. She was the backbone of our family; we all loved her for who she was, but she also came with a lot of bumps and bruises.

Sometimes you just have to face the cold, hard facts about your past and make the necessary improvements for today. You want to help the next generation not face the same issues. My mother became the parent she always wanted to be and is now forging relationships with her grandchildren in the manner she always dreamed of. You can't change the past, but you can damn sure learn from it and choose to be better.

I want my family and future generations to know you can be successful on the right side of the law. Raise your kids in a manner that challenges them when they are wrong. Support doesn't mean you coddle them and allow for the same behavior over and over. Instead of bailing them out, let them find themselves out of their own hole.

Loss teaches you a lot about life.

Obviously, when my parents divorced, I had rebellious years with some friends. My folks were very strict against alcohol and drugs. Drugs were never going to be in play. Now, with most teenagers back in the '90s? It was: "Where's the party at?" Late-night house parties, bonfires, toilet papering the home of our favorite senior teacher—those were the days.

All of this is to say: my parents are my heroes. When they are called home, the one thing that won't cross my mind is whether I made them proud. They show me that with their love every day.

Remember that small town in Southern Indiana where I grew up? We made global news! There were so many new cases of HIV popping up that the town became famous. (Infamous.) It made the front page of Yahoo News. There were so many people sharing needles that it caused an influx in the spread of HIV. It got so bad they had to call a state of emergency just to curb the transmission. It's that type of abuse that drove a good town to the brink.

Looking back, my life might seem like a made-up, Jerry Springer-like episode. But that kaleidoscope of events taught me a lot. Things change, people change, the fairytale happiness of your youth often gets replaced by the harsh reality of the world around you. Change. It's hard to accept sometimes.

* * * * *

Another hero of mine is James K. Burrell. I met Jim the summer I turned sixteen. The summer before, my parents signed a waiver that allowed me to take a summer youth job helping out with the city parks department. At the time we had about four or five parks where they would pick a small group of high school kids to help with the upkeep.

The first year I worked there, well, our boss was not the brightest. He ended up stealing all the mowing equipment and tools out of the work shed. Mind you, everything had been properly tagged as "property of city parks department." This guy eventually was caught because he decided to leave the equipment out in his front yard one day for someone to drive by and see. The rest of that summer our group went without a supervisor. We did a good job, but as kids we weren't really going to work hard on our own.

The next summer I got picked up once more for the job. This felt pretty good, because not everyone got to return. The morning of the first day I noticed a new face within the group of older men; we had a new supervisor. I ended up getting the assignment of Lake Iola, which was the mayor's park. But I got put with this five-foot-four 78-year-old World War II veteran. He was bald on top, which was usually covered with an American-themed hat, and the sides of his hair were white as snow. He had a tiny pot belly, but he was rock solid, a testament to a life of hard work.

I was also paired with a new crewmate; his name was Steve. Steve was a popular kid in school, always dating the prettiest girls. We couldn't have come from more different worlds. Steven's family was extremely successful, and his goal that summer was just to earn enough money for beer when he went off to college.

Steve and I didn't realize this little old man was about to bring us together by working us into the ground. We started on one end of the park with weed eaters, and we would just start following him as he rode on the mower. After a few hours of this, he called us over for a break. Steven tried to break the ice. He was good at things like that: starting conversations to avoid any more work. Only, on this day, Jim wasn't in the mood for pleasantries.

In fact, every day for about two weeks was pretty much the same way. If you didn't show up on time, Jim would make you sit in your car and wait thirty minutes before you could start working. This wasn't a joke for him; he was there to work. Those summer days got hot. "We don't worry about the heat," Jim would say. "It all pays the same." "What do you mean?" Steve would ask. "It pays the same to sit around too." Jim would laugh at that one, then add, "Yeah, but we are going to work."

In the mornings we would go to war on these public bathrooms. Cleaning a public restroom, especially at a park, will challenge your grit. Each morning we took turns rotating, sort of making a game out of it: who was going to get the worst bathroom? Who was getting the surprise today? Sometimes it was just god-awful, so foul, what we were cleaning up. This was one of Jim's favorite things about the job: bathroom roulette. He would burst out in the biggest laugh when we would rush out gasping for air, knowing we got a good one that day.

"Germs won't kill you," Jim would say. "If they did, I would have died years ago." Jim didn't care where we came from; he treated Steve and I like equals. He would also jump in from time to time, join in on the massacre that was those bathrooms. "Scrub this way, not that," he would say. Sometimes he would hedge bets that these bathrooms were all in our heads. I remember one morning he got an extremely nasty one. This time, foul play was involved. They broke toilets and smeared feces on the wall. Jim would talk about how it took a sick individual to do those types of things. He would talk about how he would love to speak to them about their actions. Jim was always leading by example.

Jim taught me so much about life through his stories. He loved the word *perseverance*, and he loved perpetual motion. Once he tried to change the blades on the mower himself. He didn't care for the delay from the city mechanic; he'd do it himself. To get the blade off, he was basically lifting his entire body off the ground trying to torque it free. Yell after yell, curse word after curse word—he was determined to get that blade. Knuckles bleeding; he didn't want any help. He wanted to prove that he wasn't going to give up: *perseverance*. When he finally freed the blade, he looked up at me, exhausted, beading with sweat. "Never give a f------ inch, you hear me?"

He often talked about the tough times, things like being called in to take care of something in the freezing rain or snow. Sometimes you're going to have shitty days, he would say. He said he knew people that sort of had a black cloud—bad luck—follow them their whole life.

Sometimes these types of lousy days turn into lousy weeks, lousy months, maybe even a lousy year. (We could all probably agree 2020 fell somewhere within that realm.) Those particular days—while not fun, while at times extremely stressful—are some of the most beneficial days. The reality is we just don't know it yet.

* * * * *

Pride in your work is something that can be detrimental to success. You don't have to love your job. But your performance shouldn't be an area of speculation, as though people have to guess at what you're doing. To work the right way is a form of respect.

This brings me to the "uniform of the day" conversation, one that always remained with me.

I had just gotten home from Iraq and was in the midst of trying to find myself. Jim was the one who simplified what I needed to do. He already knew I was a hard-nosed worker; heck, he was responsible for creating that in me. He challenged me and taught me that way.

So Jim saw me after my return, and he said, "You take a lot of pride in that uniform, don't you?" Of course, I told him. I earned it. "Good," he said. "Treat every employer you ever have with the same energy."

I had a simple question in return: "But what if I don't feel the same way about that employer as I do the Marines?"

Jim scoffed. Doesn't matter, he said. That employer is who you chose to work for.

Jim came from an era cut from a different cloth. You see, he was loyal to AT&T, a company he was employed by for more than forty years. He maintained cable lines from Buffalo, New York to Key West, Florida. He was a laborer his peers and company could trust.

Jim was saying: you gotta take pride in your work! This company you work for, they have a brand, a company flag. Carry that flag the same as you would carry the American flag in battle. Head held high and proud. That product or service is created on a dream, and through the passion of, those company owners, and they are trusting you with their dream. So wear it proud.

It's those messages, and those lessons, that have shaped my mind and turned me into the man I am today. I take pride in any company I work for, and I treat it with the same respect as any flag I've ever carried. This principle is important to me.

The last ten years of my life, I've been a remote employee. I am fortunate. You cannot be successful in a remote environment without having a strong work ethic, one that your leadership can trust.

Jim and I were decades apart; however, this older man became one of my closest friends on earth. I could confide in him without expecting judgment. That doesn't mean he didn't offer his opinion if he felt there was a bad judgment. When I couldn't get access to credit, Jim cosigned on my first loan. He trusted me enough to put his own credit at risk. I have been banking with that same establishment for more than twenty years. Jim was amazingly loyal.

He told me, "You are no risk at all. You will pay it back. I'm sure of it." As the years went by, we would visit, and our talks were important. I enjoyed his company; you never walked away from Jim and Jane's house without stories. They were full of them. He would always ask me about work. How much money are you making? I was so proud to share once I had started earning more than six figures. Boy, he said, that is truly something. What happened to that young boy who was working for six dollars an hour, fussing about those bathrooms? He laughed before turning to a serious look, a look that said: I am proud of you, Josh! God, I miss Jim saying that.

Jane would say Jim hung the moon. That's how much he meant to her. That's how much he meant to me.

The pandemic caused a long period of time to go by without seeing my friend. In June 2020, Jim turned 98 years old.

Life had finally caught up with him; he finally began to show his age. The man was literally jumping over bushes well into his eighties and working 40-hour weeks into his early nineties! The parks department's director wanted to honor Jim, so he planned this giant drive-by birthday celebration. Nearly a hundred cars, fire trucks, and military honors drove past my friend.

Our car was one of the last in the caravan by design. It had been several months since I saw Jim, and I had missed him so much. Just as I pulled up, I let out this giant yell: "Hooooooooooooooooo!" It was the famous "get to work" yell that Jim would holler to start our days. When Jim yelled, it was time to get out of our cars and go to work. So, as I pulled up that day to honor Jim, he started to yell, "Hooooooooooooo!"

His friends and family began to laugh. They hadn't seen him act this way with anyone else. His daughter asked if it was me, and then confirmed that with Jim. He said, without hesitation, "I know who that is. That's the boy I used to yell at to get his 'hooooooooooooooo' in gear." Everyone laughed.

We played off one another. I was a mess; I had tears flowing that were mixed with joy. He looked so good—strong like I remember.

He looked me in the eyes, held out his arms, and said, "Come here, buddy. Come on. I want a hug." And it was in that moment that we shared our last embrace, our final goodbye.

"How could all these people come here just for me?" Jim asked. I answered, "You are the greatest person we have ever met. That's why."

My friend passed away three weeks later. I knew at some point the day would come; Father Time is undefeated. But

Jim lived an amazing life. Jim said that his heart was full; that's the way everyone should feel when they pass. *Full.* A life that means something.

His impact on those around him is what will carry on. The remainder of my life the story of James K. Burrell will live on.

CHAPTER THREE

The Crucible

Structure is important for most people even if they don't realize it; this is something we have been discovering during the pandemic. As I write this book, in 2021, the nation has gone through an unimaginable shift. It's been a period where many have struggled with isolation and depression. The structure that comes with going to work and being able to regularly go to public places, like churches and gyms, was removed. Many businesses were (or are) shuttered, and states were (or are) locked down to varying degrees to help combat the spread of the COVID-19 virus.

When I left the military, I also left behind the structure that was inherently part of my military life. When you're a civilian you can structure your own day your own way. When you're in the military you get really good at following the orders handed down to you. Suddenly, those directives are not there anymore, and you can find yourself feeling aimless and lost. For me, my work continued to give me structure.

When my grandparents died, I felt the need to speak, and did so at my grandfather's funeral. One thing I have learned is the folks who speak at funerals do their best with very little substance or stories. With the younger generations of our family processing tough loss for the first time, they needed a positive role model. I decided I want to be that person for them. Even if only in the back of their minds, even if only subconsciously, I wanted them to see our lives matter and know that they too can choose an honest, positive life. That's what our grandparents would have wanted. Even when being born into adversity, you can still chart your own course and sail your own ship. I wanted to be a strong figure, step up, and pass wisdom down.

You don't get ahead in life without a strong work ethic. We live in a country that allows us many freedoms and opportunities. You can be anything you want in life, but you've got to put the work in. This is from many lessons learned, and also from that proverbial school of hard knocks. And from the Marines. There's no shortage of that lesson to be learned there, too.

When I saw the Twin Towers fall in 2001, I just knew the Marines was my next step, my destiny. I had wanted to join for a very long time. My mom didn't want me to go that route, but after seeing those towers fall, I knew it was what I had to do. So I signed up just after and shipped out for boot camp in November 2001.

My journey to boot camp was a bit of a blur. I had gone to a Nickelback concert with my best friend and a couple of other buddies and stayed up pretty much the entire night before leaving—that was a stupid mistake. The next day I flew out of Indianapolis, where I had spent the night in some lousy hotel and woke up at 3 AM to catch another flight to O'Hare in Chicago. Once at O'Hare, bleary-eyed, sleep-deprived, and famished, I spied a few of those airport pizzas and scarfed them down. They didn't stay down long. I ran for the bathroom. Great start, huh?

My stomach was in knots and my heart anxious. I hadn't flown much in my life, and the reality that I was really about to go to military boot camp was starting to set in. From my flight I saw the beautiful lights of San Diego below. *Here we go*, I thought, as we landed with a thud.

I stood there and waited for a few hours; it was super late at night. A few of us were corralled there, just waiting in the darkness. My stomach rumbled. My heart beat hard.

We got on the bus; I remember that bus driver telling us to keep our heads down. Once we entered the base, and the bus parked, my life changed forever. A drill instructor stepped on that bus and began to yell some things. I was so tired his words didn't make much sense, but I remember thinking this: *Oh my God, I did it now . . . What did I get myself into? . . . "Yes, sir!" "No, sir!" . . .* Whatever you do, keep saying "Yes, sir!" "No, sir!" As soon as we stepped off that bus, there were more drill instructors gathered around, also yelling at us: "Get off my bus! GET OFF MY BUS!" There was so much yelling.

They ushered us off and onto these yellow footprints. Side by side, we stood on our spot, and they immediately launched into the first three articles. We recited them back. The first is how they prohibit AWOL. The second: it's about military conduct, about how you're prohibited from disobeying. And the third: they forbid you from disrespecting a commanding officer's orders. As we stood there reciting all these things, we didn't really understand what we were saying. But as our unified voices saturated the night air, for the first time together, it really started to soak in: This is *real*.

Right off the bat the lessons began, starting with our feet on those yellow footprints; they showed us how we were going to be standing at attention. These footprints are perfectly spaced. Your feet are at that perfect angle; everything's for a reason. It's all broken down by the numbers. You don't realize it at the time, but how you stand on those footprints is how you're going to be standing in formation, a cohesive unit going forward. These drill instructors are just so intense; it's so surreal. The reason they call the Marines "The Few and the Proud" is because they only have about 180,000 active duty members at one time. It's not for the faint of heart.

So, standing there in formation, and without moving my head, I looked at the other recruits down the line to my right (through my peripheral vision) and to my left. I realized we weren't all going to make it through. I doubted myself at times. What was ahead was going to hurt. But I was determined. Earning the title of United States Marine is something I'll always cherish.

You may think you're headed into a real challenge, but nothing can prepare you for the experience of boot camp. From the time your feet step off the bus, it's nonstop for the next twelve to thirteen weeks. So that first morning, still on an empty stomach and dazed from lack of sleep, they whizzed us through room after room and piles of paperwork. Then there's the issue of the haircut.

Not a pleasant experience.

There's just a line of dudes, a chair, and this barber who has one mission in life: to take away every last shred of individuality you walked in with. You have a seat, there's no cape to keep the hair off, there are no pleasantries exchanged. This guy is going warp speed with the clippers like it's his reason to live, shaving heads down to the nub. That stuff hurts.

After you've parted ways with your hair, it's off to get camouflage, or, as they say, cammies. They're shuffling everyone around and using all this Marine Corps jargon. You're exhausted, hungry, confused, everyone is yelling, and suddenly words don't mean what they did yesterday . . . Windows become *portholes*. Beds are no longer beds; they're now *racks*. Flashlights become *moonbeams*; there's so many different things you've got to pick up on. They search your stuff for contraband and you're starting to figure out it's probably going to be easier to complete this than it is to try to get out of it. Like you're already here, they've already got you.

And then there's the shots . . .

I remember walking into this building and seeing a little stainless steel table, just full of these pre-filled cartridges of whatever they're getting ready to inject into you. And then you feel this prick in your left arm. As you're walking, you're getting poked. It's like you're running a gauntlet of injections. Then you arrive at the final station. You're there in your skivvies and they just reach over and pull your ass cheek out. You're shimmying down this wall with a bunch of other guys and just getting poke after poke. I don't know what the final shot was, but it felt like it was the biggest needle I've ever had going in my body. And it went right into my right ass cheek, and I swear they were squeezing the contents of an entire jar of peanut butter into my ass. That's what it felt like. *Thick.*

It burned; we bled. You stay in those skivvies for a couple of days; everyone reeks. The instructors love to play games. I remember someone got in trouble and they called everybody to attention and told us to take off our skivvies and pass them to the right and put the "new" pair on. Just as we're starting to put that underwear on, he looks at us with this look like: *Don't mess with me again.* The thought of having to put on another man's bloody underwear . . . it's just like, *wow.* Ninety percent of the Marine Corps boot camp for me involved mental toughness.

Drill instructors are a different breed. Entirely. You love them and hate them at the same time. They've got so much passion for what they do, and they're there for a reason: everything they do just intentionally stresses you out. And that's the point. They're preparing you for the potential stressors that lie ahead—yes, including combat.

The yelling . . . these guys yell to the point that their voices are going in and out. They sound like frogs when they do that. These guys are fierce, and they take it out on everybody. It's a rude awakening. They break you down to build you back up again—better, stronger. Everything that happens somehow reinforces what the Marine Corps stands for: Honor, Courage, and Commitment. They push you to your edge so that the Marine way of life becomes your first instinct, your natural way. And once you are finished, you'll continue living your life in that manner.

The methods seem harsh but that harshness is the tool they use to prepare you so that your enemy doesn't make it home— but you do.

In boot camp, you move with urgency everywhere you go. They're going to change the way you brush your teeth. They're going to change the way you shower. They're going to change the way you eat your food. You're going to grab a cup of water, and you're going to grab it with two hands and drink it.

Little by little, they strip you of your weakness, they strike out everything they consider "nasty little civilian attributes." That mental breakdown as an individual shapes you into an integral part of a moving team. You practice moving and running: everything in formation, as a platoon. Day by day your individual identity fades away a bit, and your identity as a collective whole grows stronger.

After a grueling day of training, someone has to pull what's called Firewatch. This is the guy who mans a station at the front of the barracks and stays guard all night to make sure no fire breaks out, and he just keeps overall security. That's another way that they really mess with your sleep schedule. Staying awake after pulling Firewatch duty is extremely rough, especially when you're in class learning Marine history, or something like it, the next day. There's really no air circulating, you get nestled into your seat, you're supposed to be learning something important, but you're nodding off to sleep—"bobbing for apples," as they say. And man, if you fall asleep in those classes, they will run you through incentivized training.

I was fortunate to be part of the Marine Corps martial arts program, a new program in which you can earn martial arts belts as a part of training. The program teaches learning various big strikes, choke holds, and other grappling techniques. You learn how to fight with knives and a bayonet of sorts. We learned how to take care of a wounded soldier in the field: the point is to never leave a fellow Marine behind. That's an incredibly important ethos of ours. Even in combat, you go back again and stabilize those wounds. You carry that brother out on your back, even if he's totally dead weight. Never leave him behind. You take care of your own.

I wish I would have been a little older so I could have appreciated it more, but again, when you're a 19-year-old kid and you show up to a program that's so structured and so detailed and so stressful, it's a reality check. It was one of the more difficult challenges I've ever endured. And yet it made me who I am. It transformed me from a man of intentions to a man of action.

We learned to function in any situation you could imagine. A lot of us come into boot camp knowing how to swim already, but you'd be surprised how many don't know how to swim effectively. I certainly wasn't a strong swimmer coming in, and I didn't yet know how to tread water for long periods of time. Essentially, you learn how to swim or sink away. I can remember during swim qualifier, rushing around putting this uniform on; it was heavy and oversized. I grabbed two left boots and had to make do.

The scenario was jumping off a high rise platform into the deep end of the pool and treading water. It was like fifteen minutes in full camouflage. And I'm treading water furiously just struggling to keep calm in my mind because, again, I'm not a strong swimmer and I've got all this gear on. You've got to become the most durable version of yourself, and the way you get there is by pushing yourself to the edge, over and over and over again, until your edges expand . . .

It's physical, it's mental, it's emotional. I'll never forget; it was Christmas. One of the most emotionally difficult parts of being in the military is being away for the holidays, away from your family. From my bunk I remember looking out and seeing the homes in the mountains of San Diego, all lit up with Christmas lights. Lying there imagining that those people were sharing meals, gifts, and joy. I was lying there listening to the sounds of Marines breaking wind or snoring in their sleep. It was tough being away from family at that time.

You don't get a lot of phone calls home. Everything's essentially scripted when you do. My poor mother kept sending me letters addressed to "Marine White." Adding little slogans like "oo-rah" or "devil dog." I hadn't earned those titles yet. So her messages were inadvertently getting me in so much trouble. I'll never forget that. They would read out that name and chuckle as they knew it was time for them to incentivize. "Recruit White! To the quarterdeck. Your momma still thinks you are a Marine!" Letter home: "MOM, PLEASE STOP SENDING ME LETTERS WITH ANYTHING THAT RELATES TO THE MARINES . . . "

Some of the guys came to boot camp with hunting experience, which wasn't always a good thing when it came to learning to shoot the way we needed to learn for combat. Thankfully, I didn't come in with a lot of bad shooting habits. In the Marines, shooting is repetitive, and breathing is shooting. When you're holding a loaded weapon, aiming at your target, it's really important to be very attuned to your breath. That was the biggest part I learned. Anytime you need to be super accurate, anytime you need to be in control, you have to put your mind at ease. You have to learn to control your breathing.

Something we say a lot in the Marine Corps: "one shot, one kill." We're not out there just spraying bullets. It's crazy how applicable controlling your breath plays into your day-to-day life as well. Never squeeze that trigger, literally or metaphorically, until you've completely exhaled. That is the point when your body has its natural resting point.

I think that's something most folks should learn before they fire off a nasty e-mail to someone in the office or say a sharp word to a spouse or child. They might want to control their breathing first. When I first got into corporate America, I had a tough time if I felt someone was being nasty to me via e-mail. I had to learn to control that impulse to retort. Breathing is a big part of controlling your actions; a few deep breaths and moments of stillness can spare you hours, even days, possibly years, of trouble. Breathing with purpose controls your anxiety, and simply put, it works in all facets of life. If you can discipline your breath, you can discipline your mind. If you can discipline your mind, you can discipline your body. If you can discipline your body, you can do just about anything.

Standing at "attention" means you are ready for anything. Your mind, your body, your will are primed and focused for absolutely intentional action. Become still so you can survive. You can imagine the reason they taught us to be super still— not even scratch your face—in total discipline. This is because if we're ever in an environment like a jungle or swamp, and you've got an enemy that's bearing down and you're concealed, the *last* thing you want to do is knock a fly off your face. You'd give away your team's position. That one movement could cost your whole platoon their lives. So you've got to learn that discipline, and there are tough habits to conquer. Marines have to be able to function when the air around them is toxic. We learn to use our gas masks.

No Marine ever forgets the first experience with the gas chamber. You're outside with your mask on and everything is fine. Then you walk in and gather around this table. Then someone ignites the gas and your heart starts to pound a little harder as you see the room cloud up. It starts to hit your skin;

it becomes uncomfortable, sort of like a burning sensation. Then you've got to break your gas seal with two fingers. And that's when the gas gets inside. You breathe it for the first time; you're starting to freaking panic. You've got to learn to clear all of that gas out and, by then, it's already affected the open skin inside your mouth. Burning, everything is just . . . burning. You're trying not to choke. The whole point is to learn to maneuver with that mask because you could potentially be in that situation for a couple of days or even longer, and you've got to learn how to even drink with that thing on. If the Marines are called to fight, somebody is going to have a bad day. You see, we have to be prepared for what our enemies are going to throw our way. Boot camp, and all of our additional training, prepared us to be effective on the battlefield.

The culmination of boot camp welcomes what's called the Crucible. After twelve weeks of grueling preparations, you set out on this incredible trek. It's 50-plus miles over the course of two and a half days up and down the mountains. For my journey it was January or February. Cold mornings and nights. So we are getting ready to load up and start this event, and we're all geared up. Everyone is stoked. This is it; this is the moment. I've worked my ass off; I'm ready. This is the last thing standing between me and earning the title.

We no more than stepped off, maybe 500 yards into the hike out, and I stepped off the edge of pavement and rolled my ankle, rolled it something fierce. I had this heavy pack on and I knew it was bad. I stumbled and the pack came shifting down; I felt the bones and ligaments crackle and pop. I picked myself up; adversity started to weigh on my mind. *I'm injured. Do I tell anyone?* I didn't want to get dropped. My family was flying out for graduation in a couple weeks. I limped along with doubt to the staging area for the event start. I tried to take my boot off when we got there, but it was already so swollen, and to top it off, I had Firewatch that night. Just great.

I'm already stressed out. No way I could let my family down. There were like a dozen family members set to come out. I could imagine plane tickets weren't cheap, and flying from Indiana to California was something they were looking forward to. That was the motivation I needed. *I can't fail now.* Like, *I've got to push through this injury. They're depending on me.*

And I remember just tightening that boot up to the point where: *I'm not taking this thing off. I'm going to use it almost like a cast and just push through.* But it was excruciating carrying all the weight of that pack, going up and down, rolling that damn ankle again and again on the rocks and going through obstacles. It was hard to run, you know? Ever been there, when you're just having to push through a hard thing but you're injured and all you want to do is quit? We all encounter times when we have to give more than we really have to give. This was one of those times.

I thought to myself: *You're not going to get there without pushing yourself mentally and physically to the limit.* And that's what the Crucible does. It's two and a half days of pushing your body beyond its breaking point.

The next morning we started off the day with an eight-mile hike and then broke off into smaller units. They had us hike some more, and then we came to challenge stations in which we had to work together to figure out how to complete a task. Once the challenge was completed, we would hike to another one, and then another. At this point, there's been little to no sleep for days. We're tired. Hungry. Our MRE rations hardly quell the grumbling in our bellies; we're burning so many calories charging through these mountains. We're wearing heavy packs and it's hard to think straight. This is the test of everything we have learned: right here, right now.

All the things that seemed so silly and insignificant—now they made sense. Like holding your cup a certain way. When you reach a point that you are so tired you're shaking, but you don't want to waste that little precious bit of water that you've been hauling in your pack; you have to conserve it. So *that's* why you use two hands: you gotta have a firm enough grip so you don't spill.

When you approach the final morning of the Crucible, you wake up for an early morning hike. Then you reach the pinnacle: The Reaper. You see, there are two Marine Corps Recruit Training Depots. Parris Island (South Carolina) and San Diego (known as the Hollywood Marines). The Reaper is unique to the west. The grade on this thing is insane; when you are already exhausted, it feels damn near vertical. It's got this worn-out beaten path, and I'm not even sure how long it is. Maybe half a mile, maybe a mile. At this point it's been days since we've slept, and we have to make it up this beast of a hill. The drill instructors become a little more motivating at this point. They're less harsh; they want you to make it. This is it. I remember the pain of each step.

It's a matter of mustering up everything I had left to give. *Just get to the top of this MF-er.* And once you reach the top, you're going through this ceremony to celebrate that you did it, and it's like they're talking to you but you're barely coherent. The one thing that stuck out to me when we were going through that ceremony was someone in our leadership saying: "Imagine being this tired and having to fight for your life on the field of battle. Imagine, instead of words, we could have bullets whizzing by our heads." That really hit home. Like most of my fellow recruits, we were exhausted, in pain, and the thought of having to fight for our lives at that very moment really reinforced what lay ahead.

You don't forget those things. You don't forget how you felt. That's why they pushed us so hard for those twelve brutal weeks. That's why we put everything on the line, to earn that title: United States Marine. That moment, right there, was a life wake-up call for me. I was like: *Wow, that's crazy. Crazy!* There was no way you could learn this lesson from a manual. This lesson had to be learned in the flesh. I stood there as they talked and let it soak in. Not their words, but the experience. The exhaustion, the pain, the elation. The victory.

Then it was time to hike back. All the way back. I felt sorry for the guys with short legs.

That's where marching cadence comes like a song on the wind to sweep you home. When they march us, it's a unique sound. Almost melodic. Voices, and the sound of boot in rhythm, creating song. You grow to crave it. It's special music to a Marine's ears. It's the song that carries you when your legs just want to crumble beneath you. Everyone needs a song to carry you on, to borrow strength from. What's your song? What's your anthem?

After we bussed back down south from Camp Pendleton, our last two weeks were bliss. The confidence of being the most tenured recruits on depot had to be noticeable to fresh recruits. Then it came: the day of graduation. They marched us around the parade deck for all the families to see. I looked over and, in front of me was my family, like ten or eleven of them, and of course you can't really cry or anything. I saw my mom. She was crying, and my dad was standing there too. That first hug after all of that is just irreplaceable, something I'll cherish forever; I felt so proud. They all kept saying I was different. I *felt* different too; something was different. I was stronger. I was wiser. I stood taller. I had accomplished a goal. I was a freaking United States Marine!

CHAPTER FOUR

No Better Friend

No matter what identity you take in life, and you will surely have several in a lifetime, it's important to know, at your core, who you are. You're not your job. You're not your role. You're not even what you've categorized yourself to be. I'm a Marine for life, yes, but really I am just *me*. The most important step of self-actualization is learning to accept your own brand. What are you really good at? What are your shortfalls? The latter one should be a longer list in scope, and for good reason. You should want those teachable gaps. People like to link their identity to things like titles, prestigious universities, fraternities, clubs, and the like, to help define themselves. But when people only find their value in something outside of themselves, they have a difficult time feeling important once they've moved on from that thing they've been so wrapped up in.

Along life's way we meet people who help shape who we are. Through shared experiences we discover who we are—together. We become better, together. We discover our identities side by side. One of those amazing people in my life is my dear friend Brandon.

Brandon is a Marine buddy who became closer than a brother to me. I looked up to him then, and I still do now.

Brandon could have been on the advertisements: "Join the Marines!" He is a model Marine: he keeps his body in top physical condition, he's mentally sharp as a tack, he's always pushing himself to become better and better. Brandon walks the talk, if you know what I mean; he models those high Marine ideals in every walk of his life. Even now his passion to serve his country inspires me. He's serving as a federal agent now, and I feel like I live vicariously—well, sort of—through his world travels. There was a period when he wanted to drag me along with him, but for whatever reason I was infatuated with the lady I was seeing, and Brandon and I didn't pursue the same path. Still, it all worked out fine. I enjoy hearing about his adventures, and when we catch up, it's just like old times. Those bonds created during our service days hold strong. Brandon is just one example that brotherly love runs deep among our small group of Radio Marines.

So much about the experience of deployment and parts of the Marine training we go through is intended to break you down so they can build you back up. Brandon and I have hit a place where the friendship has been so refined that all that's left is the buildup, the support, and the love. We've been through hell and back—more than a few times. Often, life within the Marines is a love-hate relationship. So much about it just sucks. But with Brandon and I, and some of our other platoon guys, the love, the brotherhood—these are the things that give us the strength to get through all the parts that are really horrible.

That process of breaking you down, like in boot camp and beyond, serves to create a sort of camaraderie that later becomes a lifeline. Guys you might not have had anything in common with or even liked in your civilian life can become your best and most trusted friends when you're subjected to pure hell together for days on end.

They say there's no better friend—or worse enemy—than a U.S. Marine.

We learn to rely on each other. It's an interesting thing; we're all pushing ourselves to be so perfect. It's competitive, yes. But there's this thing where our identities are breaking down as individuals and being built back as a group, as a force, and in that you don't have to worry. You can have faith that you can take those big risks because your brothers have your back. This is one of the things that makes military leadership so important in the workforce, the idea that you give so much for your team, and when everyone is giving together like that, the whole is greater than the sum of its parts. When there's that sort of trust, great things can happen.

You never leave a Marine behind whether he's dead on the battlefield, hurt, or injured.

The core of that feeling, the pride and fellowship, that loyalty that we share among one another, it pushes you forward when you simply want to quit. You can't let your brothers down. You're not able to choose your family in the military. And you're not really able to choose the war that you serve in and fight in, but the guys you get to go in with, all differences aside, they become your lifeline. Nothing else matters but supporting each other. Political ideas, religious background, where you come from—none of that matters. Knowing some-one has your back like that is a tremendous thing. It's healing. It's freeing. And the loyalty endures.

There's no "former" Marine. Once a Marine, always a Marine. And there's a reason for that. We're a very small part of the U.S. military, but we're the first to fight. The nation is counting on us; our brothers are counting on us.

We are very fortunate. The intimacy that we shared with one another? I realize not all men get to experience something that intense, knowing that someone has your back like that. I don't speak to these guys as often as I would like, but they are still a huge part of my life and I speak about them often. And I know if I ever needed something from them, or vice versa, we can call on each other anytime.

The trials we face together extend through basic training, through active duty, and even as we transition back into civilian life. Being away from our families, our parents, our girlfriends and wives. There are the "Dear John" letters that come while you're away that can be so crushing. You're out there working your ass off and sometimes the girls back home . . . well, they're cheating. Or other sorts of tragedies strike while you're deployed. Life goes on without us while we're away; things change. We support each other through all these trials. You can be out there running and your heart is just breaking, you're just trying to breathe, just continue on, it's so hard on so many levels. You're thinking: *I hate this. I hate running. I hate not sleeping. I hate the cold. I hate this shooting all day. I don't hate being a Marine, but damn . . .*

So we're doing all that type of stuff that we don't like, away from family and friends and those we love. We're going through a whole phase of life together. It's a common pain we all share, and we all become stronger at the end of those things. We're all sacrificing something.

There was a time when my initial training was completed, and I began to transition into the reserves, thus reaping the benefit of both worlds. For three weekends a month you get to be a citizen again. If you are totally active duty, you're in that life twenty-four/seven, getting burned out. So we come in one weekend a month, and we'd just be locked in. We trained our roles. For me, as a radio operator, it's just studying up, refining that job, and we were proficient at it. Life was going along well.

And then, after my third or fourth drill weekend, they called us in. I remember having this eerie feeling that something's about to go down. There's murmuring, there's a lot of formalities. They call everyone to attention. You never forget these words: "As of Zero-One Hours last night, your unit has been mobilized and will serve in direct support of Operation Enduring Freedom." Then I zoned hard. "You have seventy-two hours to get your affairs in order." This was a Friday afternoon. We had to report Monday.

A weekend is not a lot of time to get your life ready for what's about to happen. I was still in my teenage years, 19! What affairs did I need to get in order? I hadn't experienced much in life, and now we're drafting our wills. Imagine that. And then we said our goodbyes, all that. Processing the feelings of leaving your family behind again, but this time it's for real. You might never see them again. They won't even be able to know where we're going. The pit in my stomach ran so deep. But this was the job, this was what I signed up for. I had been called to fight.

I remember a speech one of the commanding officers spoke. He said something similar to this: "Take that scared feeling you have and that anxiety, and bottle that up. We're going to need it. You're going to use every ounce of it. You're going to call on the brothers to your right and left when you get low, and you're going to pull each other out." I was 19, standing there, knowing there was like a 50/50 chance I might die on this mission. And amazingly, all my brothers, we all beat that death—together. Amazingly, everyone in our platoon came home.

"Together" is how we got through it, and together is exactly *why* we got through it. I remember this exercise we took part in down in Fort Knox. It was raining the entire time. It was storming hard and temperatures were low. Our tent was in a puddle and it was freaking freezing. We didn't really have the best cold weather gear, just the Gortex outers that had been issued, and we had our fellow Marines. I was like, "OK, we're gonna get warm. Come here, Brandon. I'm gonna be the big spoon." That's intimacy right there; surviving together. I've cuddled with my fellow Marines like our lives depended on it. And they did.

When your life depends on cooperation, you discover the value of leading by example. If I'm going to give orders, I'm going to be out there helping too. If you want to lead and you want people to follow, the best way to do that is by being the change you want to see. You want to get the job done quickly and efficiently? Model it. Walk the talk.

They say Marines can take the uniform off, but what's changed on the inside remains forever. Even now, when I see another Marine out somewhere, even if I never knew him before, there's a bond. We are united, every Marine who has come before us, and every Marine who will be. We share an identity and a bond. Knowing we would lay down our lives for each other, for our nation, knowing we share the same ideals and ethics, even if we have nothing else in common. That's unifying.

In the Marines there's a concept called "JJ did tie buckle." It's an acronym that stands for: Justice, Judgment, Dependability, Integrity, Decisiveness, Tact, Initiative, Endurance, Bearing, Unselfishness, Courage, Knowledge, Loyalty, Enthusiasm. These are virtues, as Marines, that we seek to embody at all times. I think that's why the Marine Corps works so well and why the bonds of brotherhood we forged are so lasting. The friction and stress that occur during the training and through the missions really weed out anyone who is stuck in selfishness. We are all yielded to the process of putting on these virtues, allowing them to soak into who we are, allowing them to change and shape us. These concepts become part of us and flavor all our interactions moving forward. By putting each other first we are able to partake in a greater glory than we could ever reach alone.

The Marines have a fierce reputation, and as a whole we are a well-oiled machine. And, for sure, I wouldn't be who I am today without my experience of becoming and fighting as a Marine. But I am still me, Joshua. I'm a Marine forever, and I'm a way better version of Joshua than I would have been without my Marine experiences. Brandon and the other amazing men who came into our brotherhood also became the best versions of themselves, and through everything that tried to crush us down, we continued to lift each other up.

We come in as Average Joes, from all walks of life and regions of the country, but we became something greater, together, and those Marine attributes stay with us long after we've left active duty or the reserves. I'm in the business world now, and I'm still living this way, leading this way, serving this way. The experiences—and these brotherhood relation-ships—changed me, forged me, created the man and leader I am today.

CHAPTER FIVE

Backbone

Fear is a natural human emotion, but facing your fears takes courage. There are moments in life when you'll need to develop a backbone to face your fears. You don't have to be a Marine to understand that growth and discipline are required essentials for life. The following traits are what define Marine Corps leadership—and these traits have taught me a lot.

These things are taught as constants. Without these, it causes the entire system to fail. We train these at the bottom, and these values will remain a constant throughout your career. It's a true bottom-up (think like the foundation to a pyramid) approach.

Justice isn't something that's talked about a lot in leadership books, but it's important to our well-being, work, and life. If you're the leader of a company, justice is important because your team members have to see the organization as fair and true. If you're the leader of a family you must instill a sense of justice into your kids to teach them what's fair and right. Justice is one often overlooked but extremely important trait that goes with honor, discipline, and hard work.

Justice is our compass, our moral high ground with which we enforce discipline. Regardless of our warrior mind-set, we must act in an ethical manner. Marines have a standard we must uphold. In a corporate setting, if employees feel they are safe to speak up, leadership will be trusted. Employees will understand how to further their own growth and find a path to promotions that is truly defined by merit and hard work. Marines are rewarded and promoted in this manner. Justice must be equal and served in the right way at the right time, and that involves a good measure of discernment. There is a time and place for discipline within the workplace, and serving in the military you become accustomed to those rules very quickly. Here's an example of the smallest detail, or rule, that's enforced. Even in a combat or field exercise, Marines are expected to uphold the grooming standard. Haircut to regulation and a clean shave. Easier said than done. In a combat environment, having a clean shave allows your gas mask to seal properly. It also helps maintain a mission-ready Marine by having proper hygiene. How well does your company handle discipline?

Judgment is important to remind your team of the mission at hand; often we must assess situations quickly. Meaning you act on an imperfect solution. This doesn't mean we didn't prepare or discuss, but we need to use our instincts, lean on our past experiences. Another trait that's critical for leaders is consistency.

Are you **dependable**?

General Mattis sent out a letter to all Marines just before the invasion kicked off. Not only were we going to depend on our brothers and sisters to our right and left, on both land and in the air, but our fellow Marines had to know they could depend on us. We were all given information on our enemy; we understood the risks associated with this push into enemy territory. As Mattis said, "No better friend, no worse enemy, than a U.S. Marine." As harsh as that statement sounds, it's critical we were all entirely dependable to do our jobs. These qualities translate to civilian life as well, of course, and in managing teams, groups, companies, or your own life.

Decisions: they have to be made. Hands down, this is my least favorite part about a corporate setting. To be an effective leader you need to make decisions. How often do we sit around in meetings or on these lengthy calls with an agenda item that continually gets tabled or pushed back? There was a time when the team I was part of kept pushing back on this one topic. Things became heated, as folks were passionate about the outcome, but each week as time passed there was never a result. Why? You can put the smartest people in the same room together, but if someone doesn't make a decision to act on, it's a waste of time. I would rather have a decent solution to trial and error than the perfect plan. My favorite character trait passed down from the Marines is the ability to make a decision. Indecisiveness breeds failure, and it can cost money, or worse: the life of someone on the battlefield. Learn to make decisions.

Semper Fidelis: "always faithful" is our motto. We also throw out the term Semper Gumby: "always flexible." You aren't always going to make the right decision. But remain flexible; stay frosty to the mission or task at hand. The ability to run while making that initial decision will allow you to arrive at the desired outcome—or perhaps something even better.

At worst, you have something to learn from. Our failures in life are our greatest teachers. I have held many titles in my thirty-eight years on earth. Son, brother, Marine, husband, dad, best man, supervisor, manager, regional VP, and now published author. The work-related titles would never have happened without calculated risks.

Perhaps your plate is full. You feel you don't have time to give your best. That is what leadership is all about, because I guarantee there is someone on your team right now looking for a way to showcase their talents. Bring them into the discussion and let them run with the task. A big mistake many leaders make is that they try to do everything on their own and, when they do, it leads to an overwhelming feeling or just procrastination.

Another trait that's important, some would say the most important: integrity.

Integrity means being a person of your word, and a true leader must have an ethical foundation to lead others. There is a lot at stake when you are on the field of battle—and the same can be said of those in the corporate setting. You are entrusted with the lives of your employees—or your fellow Marines. The mission or job will fail if you don't have their trust. We are taught to gain confidence in our decisions as early as boot camp. We build trust and cohesion within our small and large group settings.

A lesser discussed leadership trait is **tact**.

The real question is: how do you handle yourself?

Marines have customs and courtesies that are taught so we carry ourselves appropriately. In a leadership position you have to be willing to deliver feedback that will enhance mission success, and that same energy needs to be invested in how we build up our teammates. Allow them the opportunities to help you grow as well by soliciting their feedback so you can become a better leader for them.

Initiative: Marines are going to take charge. We have an uncanny way of assessing a situation, creating an action plan, and delivering a result. If you have a veteran on your team, there is likely no issue with them taking the initiative on a certain project. When I was working my first summer with Jim, one of his favorite quotes was: "It pays the same." We have a job to do. We all know what needs to be done. It doesn't matter how quickly we complete it, or how long it will take, as long as the work gets done: it pays the same. Often we were looking to get done the fastest. It was hot outside and we weren't looking to be holding that weed eater all day. But what we found was if we took our time and did the job right, well, yes: the work still paid the same. However, the quality improved and we didn't have to revisit the task as often.

Endurance: this one essentially speaks for itself. When you think of the Marines, or any branch of the military, you think of athletes. Marines come in all shapes and sizes. We are taught to enhance our physical endurance, but it's also extremely important to have mental toughness. Are you prepared to take another life to defend your country? We all took that oath, but are you ready, when the chips are on the table, to fight? In boot camp our drill instructors were there to shape our mind. Everything about my time in the Marines was mentally stressful. From boot camp to rigorous combat training to radio school to learning how to become proficient in my military occupation of radio communications. And, of course, the war.

They're tough on us emotionally to prepare us for what lies ahead because we are the first to fight when the world needs us. Marines lead by example, and we have to have enough endurance for one another. Having that competitive endurance and tolerance for stress is what allowed me to secure some promotions early on when there wasn't that typical backing a recruiter might be looking for to fill the vacancy. I was able to lean on my experience and share my ability to adapt in those tough situations to secure promotions and advance my career.

I would be more than happy for my children to embrace the qualities it takes to become a Marine because those qualities will prepare them for life.

Bearing: Marines are taught an important lesson about keeping their bearing. It's more than keeping up with the appearance. A loss of bearing in front of your peers shows a form of weakness to whatever mental discipline you lack for the day. When you show up to work, check your attitude at the door. That mental edge or bearing is critical to troop morale and mission readiness. We practiced standing at the position of attention to teach us to control our movements. A loss of bearing by so much as scratching your face could compromise your location and allow the enemy the upper hand.

Unselfishness: when you sign up to serve your country you solemnly swear to protect the Constitution of America from all enemies foreign and domestic. Marines are groomed into warriors; we are feared by our enemy. The Germans coined us "devil dogs" during WWI for our ferociousness on the battlefield. For as much as we are feared, the mind-set we have within our Marine spirit is to lay down our life for our brother. No Marine is left behind. You are ready to jump on a live grenade to protect those around you. It is odd in today's climate to hear a young person downgrade our country or display a lack empathy for those who have fought for or possibly given the ultimate sacrifice.

The greatest thing to come from 9/11 was how we as a country rebounded on 9/12. Those attacks left a proverbial hole, but that American spirit quickly returned. What do you see, or what do you feel, when you see an American flag? For me, it's hope. Having served in a combat role, I missed everything about home and our little town. Sure, our country and the place I grew up in are not perfect; we are riddled with issues and at times divided. But in my honest opinion, we still have the greatest country in the world, one I would unselfishly lay my life down to defend.

In Iraq, I ran across this Scripture, from John 15:13: "Greater love hath than man than this, that a man lay down his life for his friends." I took that to heart, and it sort of explains my passion for life. My purpose. I am someone my family, my friends, my Marines, and my coworkers can depend on. How about you? I ask this question because each and every day we should consider its answer. Are you dependable? Can people count on you? This is important because without that foundation there is nothing.

Courage is yet another great word. Often we label someone as having courage if they are willing to stand up to fight. What happens when you need that moral courage to speak up when something isn't right? Do you have enough invested to share your passion? This goes back to the leadership trait discussed earlier. Making decisions in life requires some form of courage, and when you teach and train as Marines everything is about building a person's self-esteem and courage to become successful. It won't often make you the most popular person in the room. But if you stick to your guns, you remain trustworthy, and your goals to mission success will rise above all other opinions.

There was a work supervisor in my civilian identity who once pulled me aside and shared that I would never make it to a manager role with the company.

She explained that she had been with the company for twenty years and a supervisor for nearly all of it. But she had lost out on multiple bids to gain a higher position. It was disheartening to hear; it truly caught me off guard because our interaction to that point had been very limited.

She was my supervisor for a short period and likely the one most critical of my work of any position I held with the company. Luckily, I had the courage to continue my pursuit and would eventually turn her words into a distant speed bump. Reflecting on that moment, I wonder how many folks might have been deterred by her feedback? How many careers stifled because of her failures? Not everyone is qualified to lead others.

Some may have strong educational experiences due to schooling and classwork, but how well are they vetted in the field? I have been fortunate to serve with both good and bad. Those are the best teaching moments. I am obsessed with observing; it's part of my journey. Being extremely observing can be exhausting and diminish a moment, but it is necessary.

It also serves as a great deterrent to the actions of bad people. I have grown to read situations and people extremely well. I know who is truly in my corner and those who are just there using me for their gain. Pay attention to who is riding with you and who quickly retreats when the going gets tough. Just because you're loyal and committed to the cause doesn't mean they are. Choose your friends wisely.

Another important trait is **knowledge**. How can you successfully lead or complete goals without knowledge? If you are not a subject matter expert, you are failing your team. In the Marines we are taught to understand all facets of our military occupation on top of maintaining our basic rifleman skill set. At any given point, if our command took casualties, it would be up to the Marines within that squad to pick up the slack. It's a bottom-up approach.

In a business setting it's equally important to empower our employees to understand the full scope of our operations. Investing that quality time to teach and train and communicate will always keep your company moving forward. When I was coming up the ladder with this health care company, we had to take a mandatory training program called ModelNetics. One theory that always stuck with me was the "Mack Truck theory." If you have all of your responsibilities and processes tied into this one person and, unfortunately, they get hit with a Mack Truck, you lose all of that experience and job wealth. It's important to standardize, document, and have a succession plan in place to be absolutely prepared for the worst. And it's important to establish excellent comms. Without communications, how can you expect mission success? Battles are crippled without effective comms. You have to be willing to communicate clearly and effectively with your entire organization so everyone is unified with the mission at hand. Whenever we became bottlenecked in our push to Baghdad, the failures came with communications issues. It was a trickle-down issue. Establish effective channels of communication.

Loyal: this is another of life's basic principles. Loyalty to yourself, your family, your company, to those working with you to accomplish your goals.

Enthusiasm: are you contagious, and does your morale entice others to boost their morale? Becoming an effective leader means you must show up ready to produce for others. It's tough being locked in day in and day out, but you have to do it.

This is one trait Marines don't lack.

We don't get along 100 percent of the time, but it's rare to find people on this earth who truly get where you come from, what you have been through, and share in a common brother and sisterhood. We all answered the call, and thank goodness for those who did. There are plenty of people who want to diminish your service by saying: "I almost joined." Let's be honest: you almost *didn't* join as well.

By definition, there are two types of people in this world. Those who can and those who will. Now that is a broad stroke; however, allow the point to stick for a moment. What are things in your life you hope to accomplish? Perhaps you want to save a little money to free yourself from some bad choices. Can you save money? You sure can. But will you? That is your choice.

If you want something bad enough you can work hard to achieve it. Trust that. It won't be easy. The journey will be painful in scope. But the end result is so rewarding. Will you take that first step to achieve your life's desires?

President Ronald Reagan once said, "Some people live an entire lifetime and wonder if they have ever made a difference in the world, but the Marines don't have that problem."

You never meet a former Marine: *Semper Fi* until we die. Then, as they say, it's off to hell to regroup.

CHAPTER SIX

Perspective

What's your perspective on life?

If someone described you today, would they say you're joyful? enthusiastic? selfish? smart? Would they remember you for your positive mental attitude or your pessimistic outlook on life?

You can never underestimate the power of positivity: positive thinking, a positive perspective, a positive goal. When you have a positive attitude, life works much better for you. Your attitude is an embodiment of your thought, and your thoughts are the representation of who you truly are. Thoughts and conscience work hand in hand.

However, in some situations, even a positive attitude may not make life so easy unless you have a fantastic team of people supporting you. One of those staunch supporters was Jim. He was my older mentor, someone I really relied on. Jim was the type of guy who would arrive fifteen minutes early and ready to work. I wanted to meet Jim's high standard because

I considered myself the hardest working person in the room. He often referred to it as "wearing the uniform of the day," a phrase I cherished and carried with me into the future.

I am always open to criticism. I believe criticism makes us better at what we do. Of course, there is constructive criticism and destructive criticism. Whichever it is, I try as much as possible to accept it. Here is one maxim I certainly believe in: if you fail at something and don't try again, you will never improve. I've met a lot of people who believe they are perfect, and so they eschew criticism and suggestions to be better. And for the rest of their lives, they are comfortable in their mediocrity. I'd never be like those people; I am wise enough to know I can never be the best at everything, so criticism—in whichever form—is welcome.

The more you try to get better and accept criticism, the more you'll be able to overcome the obstacles of mediocrity and improve yourself. This is a maxim that is always taught in the Marine Corps, and I've gained many lessons from these teachings.

I strive to be that 80-year-old version of myself. I'm always trying to beat the odds, to be different, to change the path my family was on. I love exploring the unexplored and standing out—doing things that make me unique, applying different approaches to things. I want to be remembered as one of the greatest people ever known—at least to those who matter most to me and anyone who is willing to listen or give me a shot. I want to be up there with them, at least. I want people to remember my name and say, "Oh, that was a great man." There are those who are millionaires, both rich in monetary value and life. They've earned the titles, but I've had many titles too. I've earned the title of a Marine and, most importantly, a father. In my book these rank high and are, unquestionably, the very best titles. These are an important part of what I want to be remembered for.

When I've finished my book of life, so to speak, that book, and everything that has led up to it, will become part of my life. But it's also a stepping-stone for me to become a great human being; that's what I'm aiming for. I've already had pleasant discussions with some of the greats. It doesn't get any better than being 15 years old and having a salty World War II veteran giving you life lessons. And if you're not paying attention to the words the great ones around you are saying, if you don't notice things about them, it's your loss. I aspire to rank among the greatest because I know what greatness looks like. I think that's powerful.

* * * * *

One morning you're standing in your kitchen feeling that death is imminent. You can *smell* it. You can taste it, feel it; you're hot and sweating. You are scared. These are all the things that constitute Post-Traumatic Stress Disorder. You are in such a highly stressed environment for a prolonged period of time, and you are feeling like you are finding it hard to breathe; you are suffocating in your own environment and everything is scary. How do you unplug that? To this day I've never been able to unplug it. I have been able to overcome hurdles that helped me reach a point where I'm functional, but I had to make that decision. I had to make the decision to put myself out there, get into the workforce, get along with people. Again, people I didn't relate to. I no longer related to my friends.

I could no longer talk to my friends about certain things, and if you go and talk to your Marine Corps buddies about it, they'll just tell you to rub a little dirt on yourself and walk away. I can't blame them. This is how Marines are trained. The entire objective is to be called to war; the Marine's job is to seek out enemies and eliminate them—nothing else is ever really more important than that. We went to bed with our rifles as if they were our wives; we were intimate with our rifles, we knew them, we polished them every day and took pride in owning them. We knew what our lives were, and we also knew what we could do with our rifles; they offered a form of comfort when we held them.

We were trained in Iraq, and so we had to adapt and embrace whatever challenges came our way; some of those challenges included acknowledging that new modern warfare is urban warfare. However, before we discuss this mission at hand, I want to establish a point that, for me, there are really two scenarios in life. This is what I believe. This knowledge is what helps me deal with stress. Everything in this world is about life and death; those are the two scenarios. Everything in life is all about death, and everything in death is all about life.

Now I ask myself: is this a living moment? Is this a moment of death? Sometimes it is hard to distinguish between life and death. Of course we all know that death is not only about not breathing. You might be breathing and still be dead—hence the expression "the walking corpse." So this crappy situation that I'm in: is it an opportunity to live? Because adding more stress to already intense scenarios is what causes the increased stressors. That's much of everyday life too. We stress a lot about our day-to-day activities, mainly about things we cannot control right now. I can't control how my thoughts are perceived. But what I can control is my output, and I know in my heart that I'm doing everything to win today. It was no different over there in Iraq. I knew I had to make it to the next stop.

I had to make it through the day so I could eventually make it home. I didn't know that back then, when I was 19 or 20 years old. I was just stressed out nonstop, and that really took a toll on me. Every day we woke up over there we were in harm's way. There is just no other way of putting it. We were definitely in harm's way. The sand over there is not just regular sand; it is extremely fine and fills your lungs and body in every hole. Then there is the heat; it felt like a blow dryer just constantly emitting warm air, even hot air. When you stepped, some of the sand was so fine it looked and felt like soot, and little clouds would come out from your boots. Then there were always things on fire. And there are studies now that we were exposed to some of these burn areas; it was the very air we breathed in. We didn't know the very air we breathed was harmful to our health.

You are, however, out there with top-notch medical care. You are out there with a corpsman who can administer aid and treat wounds until you are able to get to safety. And— lord, this is important—we prayed that we didn't run over an IED. This too: you'd be driving and you'd come across trash in the road. You wouldn't have any idea if someone had buried an IED under there with the intention of blowing you up. Everything is a risk; wherever you go, whatever you do, you know deep in your heart that your life can end in a moment. It does not matter what you do or where you go; nothing and nowhere is safe.

In other cases you could be shot by a sniper just by crossing the street alone or hit by nearly anything, including a rocket-propelled grenade (RPG). The guys were dying almost every day over there. That was the life I lived for six months. No, my deployment wasn't very long, but it was intense.

Iraq in itself offered unique challenges. The enemy became cowardly. We also had enemies that were coming from outside Iraq; some were from Syria. Their major purpose was to enter the country and just kill as many Americans as they could; they were dressed in civilian attire, so it was hard for us to identify them. We were practically walking among these killers that were mixed with the ordinary people. They were warehousing weapons in schools because they knew Americans would not target schools; they also made use of the hospitals. So here you have what we considered friendlies. They'd come out during the day, dressed as farmers, and they'd take pot shots at Marines and soldiers. And then they'd get back in their trucks and carry on as if they were just out doing simple farming jobs. Nobody could suspect them because they always appeared as innocent as they could. There were also language barriers, but some of them were just devious. Academics among them would pretend they didn't understand English just to put us in the dark, and these people always spoke in their local languages whenever we were around. This was, quite honestly, always annoying. Of course, there were interpreters, but they were common Iraqis trying to make money. So they would interpret to us what they were told to tell us. And the majority of them were scared for their lives to go against the powerful men among them. You'd ask them questions and they would be reluctant to reply because they didn't want their heads chopped off. Talking to Americans—that alone—might have cost them their lives and the lives of their families, so most of them tried to avoid us as much as possible. Only the very discreet and desperate would relate with us. But it was hard trusting any of them because some of them might have been planted to communicate with us just to get information.

At one point we were going from house to house, door to door, and that offered high-stress obstacles. We were like a colony of ants walking in a community of chickens. But we had our orders: we have to clear every corner, we have to check every room. We had to be extremely vocal in our communications. But the enemy always had us in their corner. We had to watch our six and twelve (military: rear and forward positions)—all the time. We had to watch our guys on the left and those on the right. In the teeth of battle there would be wounded civilians who would run up to us seeking help. We'd try to help them out, of course, but most times it was futile; a lot of them died anyway because their wounds were too severe to survive. There were often screams of pain that preceded the inevitable mortality.

For us, the pain of constantly being on guard trumped all other pains. We were always trying to stay alive while searching for enemy combatants.

Most times these enemies would be observing our business from afar. They would be watching us, waiting for an opportunity to strike when we least expected it. Not much sleep happened over there; you'd sleep for just a couple of hours and then get up. But you were also trained for this, so you knew you shouldn't complain.

If you talk about an average American's day, there are many things we see in day-to-day life. There's a lot of stuff I've hidden from my wife in terms of stress and money. When we first started out I was making eleven dollars an hour; we were recently engaged and living in a 900-square-foot home. And then I've got a kid! Like, we were struggling. But even these struggles are not equal to someone living in a third-world country. Americans do not fully understand how good we have it here.

Obviously, my struggles filtered down from anxiety. There are levels of stress and anxiety. We got our tickets to fight, and every living, breathing moment over there was being aware of our surroundings, just trying to keep our heads because our job over there was important. This wasn't a field of exercise anymore. In reality, we were there to be radio operators and riflemen. That was it. If the comms went up, there were no "good job" hats given out, because you don't win awards for communications. But without good communications, you're not going to win anything. Eventually, after the dust settled, I did receive an award, Certificate of Commendation. Not too many guys within our platoon received those, so it felt good to receive that award for handling myself appropriately over there.

I think you can look at every facet of our lives in that way. Communications are important, whether they're on the basketball floor or the football field; calm communication is everything. And over there we had to make sure we worked in the night since we were doing crypto changes. With these encryption devices, we all had to carry them around in our cargo pockets. And every night you'd have to go around and make sure the radios for the platoon or the unit had the proper encryption code. That's a lot of stress. You had to have a secret security just to carry that thing. Having a secret security clearance with the Marine Corps? In another sense, that's a pretty cool accolade. Carrying a radio? You have to have an antenna on your back. So if you're an enemy sniper or you're an enemy that knows anything about troop movements, you're going to aim for, you're going to answer, that guy with a 15-foot whip on his back. Or you're going to target the area with the motors of the antenna, hoping you knock out the communicators.

Good leaders understand communication is going to be paramount in a mission, and it certainly has played out in war, in my house, and at work. Even the tough discussions matter. Sometimes I would get angry with my partners, especially during important matters; some of them would moan and groan. Of course, at the end of the day we are all human, and you have to learn to accept the good and the bad; that's growth. And I guess that's the difference. There were, and are, people who do not get along well with me, but I always had their backs. In the field we were nothing but brothers; personal sentiments were cast aside. So I trust them as brothers even though we might have our individual differences. What mattered was that taking care of one another was paramount. If there's somebody in your life you don't get along with, would you trust that person when you realize that, nine out of ten times, your life might be in their hands? Probably not. And that's because a bond has not been established between you.

Ninety-nine percent of the time we're not in a life or death scenario. But in a combat scenario, it is just that, and I knew the Marines had my back. It was that type of bond that had been created. That's what drill instructors make sure of; they weed out the weak-minded, those who aren't ready to sacrifice their lives for their brothers and sisters. That's what it truly is to be a Marine. It's all about sacrifice. We don't leave people behind.

I experienced something like that again recently. Someone I had trusted in without wavering decided to do what's best for them and leave me behind. It was a good life lesson and reinforced why the Marine Corps bond is different.

* * * * *

I've experienced a lot in my lifetime. That includes wearing chemical suits for months on end and not showering for months as well. Showering: I think sixty-two days is what I had marked on my calendar. It might even be more than that. I don't really know. I hadn't showered in a long time. Think about it. Your body goes through this strange metamorphosis where you're nasty—not to mention the heat of that place, over a hundred degrees. Then mix that with the gnats and other swarming insects. The heat literally felt like being trapped in an oven, and you had all this extra gear on. The layers didn't help with the heat either; we wore a flak jacket, but mine didn't have armor plates in it. We slept on or near or underneath our Humvees, which were green and had mesh doors layered with sandbags to stop an IED or some type of other explosive device. There were things that could have been logistically better, but we made it with what we had. Those were the challenges we faced, and they made us stronger, and I was able to make use of that strength. Because of it, I was able to take feedback to our unit. What could we have done better? Obviously, we found out: we need to make sure we get our guys out there with proper equipment.

* * * * *

I returned home around Father's Day 2003. Then the Fourth of July happened. There were people shooting off small firecrackers, and the cheap ones sounded exactly like small arms fire. I remember getting out of the car to, quite literally, look for cover. That was after someone lit off firecrackers in the middle of the night. I remember waking from a dead sleep unaware of my surroundings. Everything happened very fast; it was reminiscent of my days in the war, and my reflexes responded in the only way they knew how to respond to such distress signals.

My girlfriend at the time had a hard time with me. She would keep waking me up at night when I was having these dreams, saying stuff, sweating copiously. Whenever I woke from terrible dreams like that I always found it hard to catch my breath. It was through this experience I eventually learned my triggers. The room was kept like an icebox whenever I slept. Each time I slept, any heat would really bother me. Everything was crazy; I was slowly turning crazy, going out of my mind.

All of this messed with me. But those firecrackers did so most of all; they sounded like gunfire. Whenever those explosions went off, I was triggered.

When I enrolled in college and moved out of my mom's, she had just bought a nice little three-bedroom house. It was like July or August. I chose to move out and live with a buddy of mine. He gave me the back bedroom, which was the biggest room that led to the bathroom. And I literally would go to school or work and then come straight back to that bedroom.

My buddy was not the world's cleanest guy. He was just a normal guy; he didn't care about laundry or keeping the house clean. He was just himself; he didn't bother to change his ways now that I was living with him. My friend was just a normal twenty-something young man enjoying the fruits of living on his own with a childhood friend. I was rarely having fun, though nobody knew that then. I was concealing my thoughts, behavior, and emotions. I would wake up, work in the house, go to school, and then return to go to sleep. That was my day, my daily routine. I consider myself a very difficult person when it comes to the way a home is kept; any form of uncleanliness or clutter sets me off to the point I have trouble sleeping. If the carpet was unswept or there were dishes in the sink I would not be able to sleep. And that was mixed with my nightmares every night, dreams in which I would burst awake in the middle of the night, sweating like an athlete. These little obsessive things started taking over my life, and they are still prevalent to this day. Everything was difficult for my household—the standards I had to have—just for me to be able to relax in my own home. It must have been exhausting for my roommates.

I'm sure it was hard for normal people to adapt to the way I used to act, the weird things I would do. And thankfully, those things aren't warping my children, but my therapist said they're like a need. Like I needed that. Life has a way of coming to a head. It was clear I was just holding so much stuff in, internalizing it, not talking about it. It started swirling in my mind. It felt like a hurricane and everything around me was turmoil. So that's my life, the terminal stuff—the past, the present, all the stressors swirling around. Whenever I'm in my house, the stress is reduced because the house is safe and controllable, and I don't have to worry about any outside stuff. There's often no need to be hypervigilant. The house gives me a kind of comfort, it saves me from the stress of my thoughts. That's a calling for me. That is peace. My home plays an important role in that. I love making the bed every day, each time we get up from it. It brings me a kind of calm. It also signals to me. Every time I make my bed I am accomplishing something. That is a satisfying thought. Military folks thrive on tasks. Big or small. We feel useless unless we are helping out, completing tasks. Employers of veterans should understand that. Veterans have a way of handling stress like no other; in fact, we thrive within challenging situations. Harness that energy to your advantage.

* * * * *

Post-war, I vowed to never choose uncleanliness again. I had too much of it during my tour in Iraq. I slept in too many ditches and among dirt in the most extreme of climates and worked too hard to accept anything less than comfort. Anything to avoid me remembering all those terrible days/ nights I had in the war? I was ready to ensure it. So when I lay down at night, I'm not thinking, *Oh, I should have done this,* or *I should have done that.*

At a point, though, everything became overwhelming. I was going through a kind of phase and beginning to have problems with my roommate's lifestyle. I began to think I should have listened to my mom when she said I should have stayed at home with her and healed. We were told we needed to talk to anybody over there in Iraq, but now I didn't want to talk to anybody. I was young. I was learning what I needed to talk about, or who to talk to in my unit. I was scared that if I opened up about my challenges, people would find out or I could be disciplined. So I kept many things to myself, refusing to talk to anyone about them. When I moved in with Zack, that's when I started noticing things were different for me. Whenever I walked into a classroom in college, people would drop their books on their desks and make those loud, sudden noises. Because of this, I started migrating to the back of the room.

They didn't know what I was going through, so I didn't blame them. I decided to isolate myself in classes; I was always alone with myself in my corner. I often ensured that there was no one on either side of me, and no one behind me. I didn't mind having people in front of me so I could see whatever they intended to do. It was people sneaking up on me from the back or the sides that, in my mind, I couldn't allow. By doing these things I was sure I had eliminated any threat that might be thrown my way.

I was always alerted by sudden movements or noises. And because of that, getting a job in an electronics store was a big deal for me, a big step. I'd have to walk up to strangers and try to advise them about what product to purchase depending on their budget. It was a new experience for me; it didn't come easily at first because I often had problems communicating with people. Gradually I got used to the job's demands. But deep down I was still nervous whenever I related with people. I have trust issues, especially with strangers. The worry about communicating with people still bothers me today.

I've got to go through my own routines. There was a particular time when we were up in Chicago for a business meeting. Dead of winter on that day, yet the meeting was set in a tiny office with the heat blaring from one of those old school radiator heaters. Trigger inbound. I had already started unbuttoning my top button and loosening my tie. I could feel the temperature in my body; it was an overwhelming sensation.

It was like it started from my feet, came up, and my breathing and heart rate accelerated. I was so uncomfortable I thought I was going to pass out. I was starting to breathe hard because it seemed like air had totally disappeared from this tiny room. It was like I was suffocating. That was when I started to feel the ringing pressure in my ear. At that moment, I told myself, I had to find a way to get my breath back. This particular attack was memorable because it came on so quickly. It felt like a heart attack; I did not fight in Iraq, I told myself, only to come home and die this way. It would be ridiculous, even highly shameful. I decided to excuse myself and get cool water, which helps with relieving pressure on the body. The water helped cool my temperature; because of this single experience I started the practice of always carrying cool water with me as a support.

Looking back now, my only regret from the war was not being old enough to appreciate it. The fact we got to participate during an invasion of another country, to see modern warfare up close and personal—it was nothing short of astonishing. I rode around with a couple of lieutenants who were a lot older than me even though they were young to be lieutenants.

They were constantly telling me that we were near historical places such as Babylon, or, "we just drove over the Tigris River"; some of these locations are meaningful places in the Bible. But it was hard for me to feel anything; I only wanted to go home. Looking back at it now, I realize I missed out on the experience and enjoyment of seeing these places. Many of these sites cannot be visited by the common person. These places are ancient, and my lack of maturity hindered the experience.

The reality was, at that point in my life, I was tired of every-thing. I just wanted to go home. There is that point in the life of almost every Marine, no matter how brave you may think you are. There will always be that moment you just want to leave everything and go home. But that's youth—the immaturity I had at the time. It was like: let's do what we came here to do so I can just go home.

That was my mentality at the time. When you're younger, you look at things only on the surface level. It's that clarity you have with age; it's that maturity where you're able to slow it down and really see and appreciate things. Sometimes you have to learn to rise above the tall grass, and you just look at the world going on around you and appreciate it. Focusing on being stuck in the mud all day long is not how to live. You're thinking: *All this sucks and no one cares.* Realistically, there is a lot to appreciate about the *now.*

One summer day I was lying in the back of the tailgate with Jim. We were avoiding our boss; we took refuge under an old shade tree. The sky was beautiful that day. Jim spoke about how lovely it would be to smoke a joint and just float among the clouds. He would say silly stuff like this often, just to soften things. He would then switch over to talking about how lucky we were. Jim understood my background and knew things were not easy, and probably wouldn't be, the rest of my life. He claimed that, sometimes, based on his life's experiences, some folks just have to work harder than others. It may seem like there is this constant black cloud always looming, hindering or even ruining the day. Jim didn't want to change the outlook or the clouds; rather, he said we should stop to appreciate the good days when they came. That's a powerful life lesson for anyone going through or feeling that they are always under a dark day. Embrace it. Those challenges are offering you experience and grit to handle things that may come.

* * * * *

I'd love to go see Iraq now compared with those times when my only mission was to fight. I hope I'll have the opportunity to return there as a tourist and see how things are, how things have changed. I'd love to relive that moment now—in a safe way, of course. It's a third-world country where there's meat hanging in the market, just meat, with bugs all over the place. That's how these folks live their normal lives. You'd never catch an American near an open meat market with meat with bugs all over it. Running water was scarce for some, and then there's the problem of electricity.

Imagine getting killed for not having the right religion. The life expectancy over there is much younger than other countries. So all of that is what these folks have to deal with; this is their reality. Think about that as a person who walks around in a free nation. It made complaining about eating MREs for months on end small in scope. Food for us, though, was just to sustain life. (I'm telling you, it's not a pleasure to eat those MREs.) But you can't complain when you see these people making do with so very little.

I don't know anybody who didn't say goodbye to themselves at some point, because you didn't know what might happen in the next moment. The uncertainty was scary, especially with the fog of war refusing to clear. You're going to have these WTF moments. Then at some point you are going to conclude that you're going to die. So that was a mind-set you had to have, you had to be at peace with that, because you made a choice. Nobody dragged you there; you came of your own volition. You wanted to serve your country; you were there for the fight. We were all Marines. That was our job, and we had to make peace with that. Like, at some point, you were telling your buddy: "Hey, I got this letter. Will you deliver it for me?" Most of us wrote letters to our families; these were letters that were supposed to be delivered if we didn't make it. I don't know a guy among us who didn't do that. So, as a Marine, you had to be prepared for the worst, you had to prepare yourself for whatever was going to happen. I don't think I ever shook that. Even to this day, it's like: oh, well, yeah, I did that kind of thing. That's how it hampered my ability to live a fulfilled life. I was stuck in the mud. I wasn't rising above the tall grass. I was tired. I was too busy trying to figure out what was on my end. We literally invaded that country, and nobody will take that away.

Something I do know is that we did some good things over there. We took weapons caches out of schools. We built bridges. We brought food to people, gave them medical care—more than they had before we took care of them.

There's something about knowing we were the first. I was part of one of the first initial ground troops in a major combat exercise. I'll carry that with me. And no, we were not asleep inside of a barrack or something like that. We slept on top of, inside of, or around our vehicles. Sometimes we slept on the ground, inside what they called shallow graves. These were big holes. Hopefully a bomb wouldn't drop on top of you, but you went down far enough in case one dropped around you—but then the shrapnel could kill you. You would also hope to God that someone didn't jump in. It would be a dangerous situation for you. They're in the foxhole with you, trying to stab you.

We were in the vehicle the entire time. We would drive, stop this mount, now get on top, now blow up stuff. All the while we had an enemy who didn't play by the rules. Now if we had to take a dump, it had to be three or four feet from our Humvees, with our buddies cheering us on over there on the side. No, Marines don't care about privacy. We were taught and trained to be aware of our surroundings. We had enemy combatants around us, including the elements, like the heat I already mentioned.

Then we had fear. All kinds of fear. Did we have enough rounds on us? When am I going to get a call home? When am I going to get some mail? I hated everybody in Iraq. I got to that point where I hated everyone.

I started looking back at some of the pictures to see some moments I captured on film and all these little white and orange panel vehicles and the overall surroundings. It's hard to imagine I took part in that at times. Over there, there were cultural differences, and how you see religion was a big thing; that sort of changed religion for me too. Like how factions of people living in the same area can be so vastly different, hating one another. It's all driven by religion. We do that in America too, even if we don't admit it. Think about it here with the recent elections; you're either red or you're blue. It's like the whole battle in time. We all share the same planet but we're all so vastly different in these countries. And just to think there's a kid who was born in the eighties, around the same time I was born, but we don't share anywhere near the same life even if we were born on the same planet.

So it was an entirely new experience for me to go to a third-world country to live a part of my life, all in the name of serving my country. I was fortunate to be a reserve and get the chance to come home. We all earned our stripes over there.

* * * * *

The battles we fought afterward were just as important. That's what this book is all about. I want someone who has gone through something tragic to read this book and walk away knowing they're going to be okay. It's okay to talk to somebody because isolating yourself from people you care about sucks.

At times, things can happen so fast. One minute you're around friends and family and having a good time, and the next you're being deployed. Then you're facing frustration. You're scared. Fear is real. You're not scared of anything—but also scared of everything. You're neither dead nor alive. That's reality in all of our lives. Like, I'm going to die, right? You just don't know when. Most people do not know when they are going to die. They're all hoping to grow into old age before they die—but still, they know they're going to die. It's inevitable; there's no escaping it. There's an expiration date for all of us. With that in mind, you may be willing to go up a hill and fight. Sometimes your enemy is visible, and sometimes the enemy is internal. And that's the battle I've been fighting for the past eighteen years of my life, the internal battle, the battle against myself. How do you enjoy life better? How do you live in the moment? Certainly children being born, marriage, weddings of friends, these are essential parts of life that one should cherish.

* * * * *

Early in my deployment a sergeant came to me while I was doing a radio watch, monitoring radio relay and traffic. One of them suddenly grabbed his patrol bag, which was a small pack containing two days of skivvies. "White, you are headed up to support forward operations, which is going to be near the border of Iraq."

It was days before the war kicked off in mid-March. So we get there. Most things there are good. It's hot, and so going up there became . . . boring. And we do some training in the day, but then based upon the intel we had, 51st Mech Iraq's first line of defense was on the other side. So our enemy was close. Thinking back, I had literally seen my family a few weeks back, and now I was on the border of Iraq, with the possibility that I might never see my family again. It was surreal. When the fight started, it was just so unreal. The first time a 50-cal went off, that was the first time I saw an explosion in a missile or artillery strike. Everything was so crazy! But we continued to punch forward; there was no going back now. *This is what I signed up for.* Our mission was in Baghdad, toppling the regime. Our larger pushes came in the middle of the night most of the time. Although it was slow and monotonous, we got there.

Our job was to eliminate Saddam and give peace to the Iraqi people. However, we knew that, in terms of a societal change, it wasn't going to happen overnight. There was going to be resistance. It was not going to be a walk in the park. We were in very dangerous territory, and there was a very high chance we were going to be wiped off the face of the earth. We were invading a country; I tried to put that in perspective. If strangers come to my house and attempted to harm me or my family, naturally I would have to fight back to protect all of us.

Go there with me at this time, using your imagination, but on a smaller scale. Imagine yourself planning to break into your neighbor's house. You have knowledge that the owner of this house has weapons, and he is more than willing to protect his home and loved ones from invaders. When we invaded Iraq, we had to have respect for the occupants of this country who were not enemy combatants but rather human beings protecting their own. To them, it was like we were breaking into their house, even though we were not there to kill innocent people.

That was not our intention. We were going there to free these people and, while the freedoms and liberties were many years away, our goal was to target the bad guys, which was difficult because they were using modern guerilla tactics. There were explosions and firefights, and we were only able to maneuver around them for the bigger task at hand. Someone else would eventually come along and engage those lesser threats.

It's amazing to me how intrigued humans are about conflict. Violence and death are relative in scope. Since the beginning of time we have fought elements, nature, disease, and one another for survival. Even in modern times we prepare and train for the inevitable. The only difference from then and now is we get to see it; the world is more connected now. Personally, I don't feel the world is any more dangerous than it was. Danger has always lurked; those who are evil at heart now simply have a much easier way to connect and unite with one another to carry out their wickedness. The world is more connected, and unfortunately we are fed information that continues to divide us or leave us in fear.

Recently I was diagnosed with PTSD and, with it, a severe case of hypervigilance. Learning about this diagnosis and its symptoms, it's been life-altering, even somewhat of a relief. It's taken me seventeen years to seek help for change. When I returned home there were short bursts of happiness, but there were also sleepless nights and isolation and fear. There was something missing in me.

There's another side to this. The war also impacted my family. My mother told me her friends checked on her while I was away. The woman was so worried she would drag a mattress into our living room and sleep in front of the TV during her off hours, glued to the text crawl at the bottom of the screen. She was hoping against hope her son's name didn't come across the screen.

* * * * *

When I came home, I don't think she wanted anything more than to have her son stay with her, but I always felt like I was going to be a burden. That's when I chose to go live with a longtime friend. So when you experience conflict and your mind and body are beginning to develop a sort of callous, the mind that develops this callous hardens, and so we don't react like normal people react. My triggers became even more minor things. There were always unexplained noises. Some triggers are known, and some are simply movements and reactions of others within your general area. Not having a true scope on a stranger around me, not having a clear point of view—well, that raised my anxiety. It's hard to stay present in the moment when you are battling the mind.

When you were over there you could pull up and find yourself near a decomposing body that was just stinking. The bugs could be so thick inside your nostrils and ears. And they're making that buzzing noise nonstop. Blood has a certain smell to it; I'll never forget that smell. Even when I think of the period when I served my community as a volunteer firefighter, I think that's part of the reason I had to step away. Just rolling up to a scene and seeing a civilian, someone's knucklehead kid who was just injured, or a guy trapped in a vehicle—and you watch that person burn alive. Some moments just felt too close to the memories I was trying to forget.

When you transition out of combat, your regular life should change. The past seventeen years have taught me that when you speak to people, advocating for change, it becomes a daily battle. When you're in combat, you develop a new type of anger, a new level of intense hypervigilance. It may never fully turn off, but you have to learn to manage it. So the question becomes: how can I use this to my advantage going forward? At a point in your life, you can use stressors from the battlefield to help you. Your ability to thrive within a surrounding of chaos is an attribute you cannot teach. So one of your biggest weaknesses is also your biggest attribute.

This is all about gaining perspective and learning how to improve. You've got to learn to curb some of the emotions and reactions. I don't recall a whole lot during certain periods since returning home; obviously, there are big moments, and I've been able to find success in the workforce. But the day my son was born, the reaction that consumed my body—I wasn't ready for it. It was not a normal reaction; it was something that bubbled to the surface. I had not felt an emotion like this—pure love—in a very, very long time. My firstborn son saved my life. He was like a blank slate. He represented the purest form of his parents, and I will never forget regaining some sense of normal life again.

* * * * *

Typically, Marines are trained to seek out and eliminate enemies. In Iraq we had to adapt to and embrace new challenges of modern warfare. Before we discussed any mission at hand, we had to know there were only two scenarios: life and death. Every day that we woke up, we lived in harm's way.

There were a number of challenges in Iraq. We were easy targets for the enemy because we stood out like a sore thumb. Our uniforms, the color of our skin, our movements—it was clear to everyone we were American soldiers. But the enemies were concealed; it was hard identifying them because they mixed themselves with the civilians.

In the area of concealment, each coalition member was provided a quick pocket guide of our rules of engagement, but this just made things extremely difficult when they were blending in.

The anxiety in me built for years. Then, when you get your ticket to fight, every living moment is being aware of living and breathing. Our job is very important because we have to maintain communication. We must continually be connected to one another. It is very important that we are able to reach each other because, without comms, it will be very hard to win the war. Communication is paramount to the success of every mission in war. Even in our homes, at work, and within our daily interaction, it's critical. Communication makes the world go round.

When I returned home from war, I wanted nothing more than to shower and remove my camouflage. But my camouflage remains to this day. I have been conditioned for battle and, for all intents and purposes, the kid in me was left over there in that desert. I left as a kid and returned as an adult.

I remember a moment when we were on a special patrol. While on this patrol, which was only to have lasted a few days, things got real and we uncovered something of meaningful intelligence. So for nearly a week and a half we had to protect this area from intruders and looters. I never figured out what we had uncovered, but, we were told, it was something of utmost importance.

Prior to the war even kicking off, and shortly after President Bush gave us our 48-hour notice, a projectile came over the line. It was quickly dispatched by our defense, but it brought the eerie call that no Marine wants to hear, the moment we donned our gas masks—and it wasn't a drill: "Gas, gas, gas!" Now we trained for this, in some way, daily. Only this time it was different; someone was sounding the handheld crank alarm, which was a distress siren to warn everyone to prepare themselves. Shit was about to get real.

The war had not even started and we were already in danger. It was an unexpected situation, and it occurred to every one of us that if we had just received a bio attack, we might not make it home. It was going to be a real shame if we died *now*. Personally, I was going to be pissed. I had come for the war, not to die in some ridiculously sudden manner.

As a radio operator, it was my job to ensure my fellow Marines received proper communications. If I messed up, a single mistake in relaying traffic might cost someone their life. So I had to be careful, knowing that I would not be able to live with myself if their deaths came from my personal stupidity. I would not be able to come out of the depression that would follow. Every pair of eyes would look at me and judge me. It would be on record that I was the soldier who caused the death of his fellow Marines because he couldn't do his job right. I could not allow that to be my identity, so I had to be extremely careful and efficient.

One of General Mattis's promises prior to stepping over the line of departure was that we need not fear; we had our battle buddy to the left and right, front and back, and in the sky. There was intimacy at a higher level, higher even than we realized at the time, and when it was over we *still* never truly understood it. But that's true with any part of our lives; you can always look back at the happiest part of your life, and it always comes down to people. Those people, at that time, played an important part in your happiness. They helped you, and those are the people you will always remember, the ones who are there when you need them most. They are the ones who pick you up when you're falling. The ones who shine bright lights in your darkest gloom. These are special people you must always cherish, for without them you'll be in a dark place. I am always thankful that I have people like that in my corner—they are genuine people, real people, not fake-ass friends. Our radio platoon was full of goofballs. Sure, some moments were just schtick, but many moments were those when we were just trying to make the other guy laugh to get through the monotony of our day.

I read something once about how, if you want to succeed, you hang out with successful people. But you have to identify what is important; those goals have to align with your personality and what excites you. I am proud to say I have served among some of the greatest individuals on this earth, both militarily and professionally. I can proudly say I am surrounded by great people who have my back.

There is safety in numbers, right? Think about it: when we toppled and invaded a country in a matter of days, it was an effort of many, a collective mind frame at work. It was not a mission that could be carried out successfully by a lone individual. Those who carried it out had to work together as one, which we did. The result was a great achievement.

Why do we warriors avoid talking about or accepting others helping us on a path to a better tomorrow? I have not won a ribbon or medal since being in Iraq; however, I woke up every single day of 2003 fighting these very real battles within me. It was a lonely experience. It was exhausting, and it got to a point where I didn't understand the chaos swirling around me from the generated anxiety or fear I was trying to avoid. There have been moments when I would bolt awake from sleep in fear. It was often a nightmare; terrible things happened in Iraq. It was starting to not only mess with my sleep but also my head.

I did my best to not let what was worrying me, what I was scared of, affect the people around me. I did not want to be a burden to anyone or be seen as pathetic. I didn't need anyone to look at me with pity. I chose to learn about self-growth. I needed to develop myself. I had to face the illness that was trying to hinder my quality of life, and I had to do all this on my own.

Back home, with hypervigilance being a very real condition, I didn't really feel comfortable within any setting outside the confines of my home. I mean that in the context of things that were, basically, uncontrollable for me. I'm aware that threats exist each day. This awareness is in my head, and I am continually planning for the worst; that was what the war did to me. I am always getting myself ready for anything that could be tragic. I don't have a reason for why I do this; I just do.

I have achieved many successes since leaving the Marines. I don't fear challenges, and when I am within a stressful situation I tend to thrive under the pressure. Therefore, my productivity and ability to maintain that mental toughness separates me from my industry peers. Anyone reading this book who has ever been in these situations, you know that you learn to leverage that strength to better your situation. Apply for that promotion; the results may surprise you. There are companies out there looking for that military grit, for that reliability that comes as second nature. You just have to go out there and make yourself known.

What I will tell you is that I am now aware I have a problem. The first step toward healing is acceptance. At least that's what I learned in my therapy. By acknowledging that there are problems, only then can one seek a solution. If you don't believe there's a problem, how would you even think of seeking a solution? It's okay to not be okay; but it's not okay to not seek a cure for an illness. There are people who refuse to seek a cure because they have learned to live with the pain. This is wrong. I know I have problems, but I must ensure they don't affect my pursuit of a better day, my pursuit of happiness.

I can even thrive in chaos. Maybe that's because of my military training, or maybe it's an innate thing in me. I learn to figure things out in high-stress situations and operate with great success. It's those quiet moments I struggle with. Silence sucks big time. As a warrior, I know I must improvise and adapt to overcome the enemy within.

I am no longer willing to camouflage my pain. Am I under construction for the rest of my life? Absolutely! Who wouldn't want to be? In life, we struggle to be better every day. We are always searching for that improvement, for success. It's important for me to figure out where I stand in this life. I need to know my identity. The things I believe in and my personal philosophies are what make me the person I am. There are a thousand other books that will inspire you, but I want this book to be different. It should stand not only to inspire you but also to make you discover who you are.

There is a distinction between *can* and *will*. Only a thin line separates the two. Can you or will you? Lots of people have the potential to do great things, but they lack the will to do it. They can, but they won't. You, as a human being, should be capable of doing what your heart desires. You must believe you can do it. My money will always be on those who are willing; they are the determined lot who will not allow anything to stand in their way of success. You can never overestimate the power of the *will*. Great things have been invented in the world through this power because people believed in their abilities to be able to make a change in the world.

Go all in. Let your will guide you. Believe in yourself—and you will be greatly surprised by what you are able to achieve. Do not let anyone or anything hold you down. Believe in yourself first, and every other thing will fall in place.

CHAPTER SEVEN

Life

As you go through life it's important to have people you can rely on. This book is my way of paying homage to everyone who helped shape my path. I acknowledge the upbringing of my parents in playing a major role in my life. Then there is Jim, who played an equally important role. These are not the only people, however. I've had mentors in the civilian force who have been marvelous in helping me in my journey through self-discovery and healing. After serving with folks like Brandon and the other guys in my radio platoon, I've come to the conclusion that they are of an extremely high caliber, or standard, of person. They are genuine human beings who were fierce warriors on the battlefield. Oddly enough, what is it about having the capability, knowledge, and willingness to end a life that is so invigorating that you choose to love someone greater than you did before? You see, war is a by-product of the times, but that doesn't mean we will wander through life with the same objectives. One of my buddies who served with me is now a state senator. So I am surrounded by inspiration, which is why I consider myself highly fortunate to have hung out with these men. The bond I had with these people was as strong as that of blood brothers.

How I feel about my brothers in the radio platoon is beyond description. You see, I was not really close to anybody I went to boot camp with. I was part of a team and I had a platoon, including drill instructors along the way. That alone is something you kind of earn—you know, like an individual award. Along the way, you also need to learn the importance of teamwork, since no man is an island, and a single soldier does not make a platoon.

When I got to Indianapolis, I was a part of the communications reserve unit. The company had quality leadership; these were guys who had been in the corps a lot longer than most of us who were considered green. It was there I met Brandon; he was one of the first guys I met. I recognized him only because he was in the boot camp with the friends I should have went with after graduation. There were some other guys who checked in around the same time. One of them was particularly older than the rest of us; we called him Old Man Moose. He was about thirty years old at the time and he came a month or two after me. He was much older, so having a 30-year-old colleague felt different to me. A lot of the guys used to harp on him for being much older than the rest of the guys within that rank. I suppose other guys in his situation would have taken great offense at all the fun we made of him, but Old Man Moose was a down-to-earth guy. He never took any offense at all the jokes, and he didn't consider himself superior to us due to his age. He was totally humble and fared well with all of us; he had so much more life experience that we all marveled.

That's what we did; we weren't afraid to get after one another. The radio guys—some of them I cannot give aliases to since they are either still serving or doing something else kickass these days. They are unique and special to me in different ways. The guidance, confidence, and inspiration they provided—I can't fathom it all. You all know who you are and what you mean to me. We are entwined for life, these battle buddies of mine; we have gone through hell and back together. Truly there are no better friends, and no worse enemies, than you!

Just a few years back we ended up losing a fellow radio guy to cancer. The guy was a fun-loving person; he was a platoon jokester and always bringing us closer together during the suck. His name was Jimmy Wags. Like my mentor Jim, they were both little guys who had sort of built towering statues to themselves. Then there were the types like our platoon Sgt. Lamb, who was the perfect poster boy for the stuff he wanted to do. His entire life was just like a machine, as if he was a robot controlled by a mechanical apparatus. We all admire and look up to the service he puts in for his country, still, to this day.

We were all guys who came from different backgrounds, but there was this unique understanding among us that it didn't matter where you came from or what race you were. What mattered was we were brothers and had each other's backs because of the bond we shared. At that point, we were each other's immediate family; we were brothers. We were as close as siblings could get. Even then we were often looked down upon by some of our superiors, like there was a stigma about us. There's always a kind of rivalry between the army guys and Marines—and we the reserves were often looked down upon. With reservists, well, not many know they are actually called upon as the first to fight, and we did our duties bravely and earned every bit of reward that came with doing our jobs well. Those inter-military beefs about what branch you served in, or if you are a weekend warrior or not, seem more like uneducated or even youthful misunderstandings of the military as a whole. Marines, regardless of whether you are reserves or not, go through the same boot camp, same school of infantry, and same occupational schooling as others. The only difference is you get to come home after, return to college, and drill one weekend a month and two weeks a year. That doesn't mean you are less of a Marine—nor did it impact our path in taking part in the invasion of Iraq in 2003.

I was always sensitive about someone calling us weekend warriors, as if we didn't matter. I know a lot of weekend warriors who went above and beyond, the ones who actually saw combat as opposed to the guys who simply went active duty for four years at a particular station. At the end of the day, we are all Marines.

Therefore, I really want to eliminate that stigma of being looked down upon or being considered irrelevant. This is another reason for writing this book. All these guys who are regarded as reservists, or weekend warriors, sacrificed a great deal of their lives. We were just doing what was required of us; we were trying to go to college and, at the same time, serving our country. And we earned a title the same way all of us went through the same boot camp. These guys were just phenomenal people. They are partly responsible for shaping me into the person I am today. I learned a great deal of discipline just by being with them. Sometimes they push you to the limits; they encourage you to be the best version of yourself. My time with them was some of the best of my life. With everything I experienced in service, there were moments I am not proud of. There were some ugly moments, and those were the events that birthed the PTSD in me. But nothing can take away the pride I have in serving with these warriors.

I dreaded going back to drill after my tour in Iraq. I was injured and had checked out mentally. I assume things would have been psychologically worse for me had I not had my colleagues to help me through those times. I owe everything to them. They helped me finish my term and made everything considerably better for me. It's like looking in the mirror; while they had their own mental stuff to battle with, they still stood by me. Because of them I was able to cope with a lot of things. In return I'm learning how to help them unlock different things about themselves that we all struggle with.

These guys—my colleagues in the Marines—know what they are doing. They are good at what they do; there is a bond among us that's unbreakable. For instance, when we go out for a run, there's always that motivating atmosphere and the feeling of comfort that you are with your people. It's like we are all in sync. We yell at each other and motivate one another to complete tasks. It's impossible to win a war by yourself, and it helps to fight a war with people you are comfortable with. There is always that calmness of mind in the fact that you trust whoever is on your left and right; you trust them to take care of you whatever you are doing, just like you are going to do the same if the roles are reversed. You are willing to risk your life for them.

A true Marine must be ready to go the ninth mile for a fellow Marine. If a grenade drops and you are the first to see it, or none of your buddies see it, and there is no time to warn them . . . you must make a split-second decision on how you're going to protect your buddies. What do you do? You jump on the grenade, sacrificing yourself so they can live. It's just a straightforward mathematical analysis. It's better for one sol-dier to die protecting the squad rather than the entire squad dying so that one person can live. If you seek cover and leave your buddies to die from the grenade, you have failed. Your failure will haunt you the rest of your life. You will be branded a coward, and you will live your days in shame because you refused to do what it takes, what is required of a true warrior.

There are many similar stories like that, of members of our military, not just Marines, paying the ultimate sacrifice so their buddies can live. I always assumed there would come a moment when such sacrifice would be required of me. I al-ways asked myself if I was going to waver if something like that took place. Would I really jump on a grenade for my col-leagues? At first I was filled with doubt, but as I studied friends and looked at the loyalty in them, knowing they would not hesitate to sacrifice themselves for me, I knew immediately I was going to make the jump without any question. Giving up my life for my colleagues would be the most honorable thing to do. I was ready to do what was required of me.

The world today is one walking on its head instead of its feet. People are so easily influenced by the news they hear, and the news of today is often a forked tongue of a snake. You may hear in today's news that something is red, then tomorrow, in the same news, you will find that the same thing has been de-clared purple. It's hard to believe what the news says anymore, at least for people who really question the logic in most things. But such dubious news is often the news people seem to swal-low because these false understandings are often salted with occasional lies and fancy words. There's always a consequence for all of this.

That's one of the great lessons I learned in the past three years during the time I decided to leave the company I was working with. Well, in truth, I just made the decision; I can't say my guts had the greatest influence on my decision. I wasn't really following anything; I was just doing what I thought was right.

You see, at that moment, I was in an awful place. It was around the time when Morgan died. It was a blow that was hard to deal with. For the first time in a long while I was trying to cope with my family—the same family I had not seen for a great number of years.

Morgan's Death—Impact on My Life

Morgan's death. I think it was this realization and the events from that day that finally broke me. I became a totally different person. In fact, it was hard for me to look in the mirror. I was scared I was not going to like the person staring back at me.

I was starting to think I had a good handle on things. I was making it. I was still suffering internally, but nobody really knew about that. I tried as much as possible to keep people from finding out about this suffering. Everything was in my head, replaying and replaying my most dreaded events. It was all chaos and commotion that was affecting my day-to-day activities. It began to interfere with my decision to lead within a company I was doing well at.

At that point in my life, I knew the right thing was to seek help. But I was reluctant. I was scared that seeking help would not only make me look weak, it would also give people the impression I was damaged. Besides, I thought I was doing the right thing, making the best decisions for the company. I didn't really interview for the job. That's another thing; I've never really been interviewed for a sales job. It always came naturally to me, either via good faith or good word or the trust of those individuals hiring me to do a great job. I have been hired by this same company twice, and neither time was I part of a formal sit-down interview. I suppose there is something in that statement alone to be proud of.

In the journey of life there will always be people who will attempt to bring you down by leading you down the wrong path. They would love to see you fail just to feel good about themselves. You will have people around you, people you think will help you arrive at your destination, but you will know the true nature of these people when things start to go bad. It is the true ones who will stand with you in the end; they are the few who will remain to pick you up when you fall. These kinds of people are rare to find. They will dust you off and give you some guidance to get back on the right path.

If you are struggling with a disorder such as PTSD, hyper-vigilance, anxiety (even terrible anxiety), depression, or you're simply stressed out and need an outlet, there are various ways you can seek treatment. My advice is do not try to manage these problems alone. Talk to people; there are those who are willing to help you back to your feet. It is not a sign of weakness to seek help. The best of us are tried every now and then. You should develop the courage to speak to someone about your problems, your challenges. A problem shared is half over with; do not attempt to deal with your problem alone. It is always lonely down there. There are professionals who can be there to help you get better; their job is to help you overcome some of the challenges you may be facing. There are therapies that will put you back on track.

It took me seventeen years to find my way to the Veterans Administration and, specifically, to find my therapist. That was seventeen years that I can never have back, seventeen years of wasted time. Do not make the same mistake I made.

Iraq was the best—and worst—case scenario for me. It was in Iraq that I learned many disciplines. Victory sometimes comes with a price. Even though I learned to be a better version of myself through the lessons I learned in my tour, it was also there where I developed PTSD, which I have battled for a long time. I endured a lot of things that would have made many other people go mad. But Iraq, in a way, was part of my identity as well; when I left, a part of me was left behind in Iraq. I could feel in myself that I did not return as the same person who left for the tour. It took something of mine that would take a very long time to regain.

By some means not yet revealed to me, I will find out how this came to be. I acknowledge that I am not totally reborn, but I am spending every waking moment trying to be my better self. I am still a work in progress, and I have come to terms with the fact that that is what I will always be. The kid who went over to Iraq was not the adult who returned. A lot of things have changed. While some lost part of me might be found, some part would remain permanently lost—and I must learn to live with this simple fact. There are things I suffer with in silence; they are things people do not know. They are so dark that I do not even have the strength or boldness to write them in this book. Maybe someday I will be able to tell them, but how many stories of woe can a man tell? Every day is born with a new challenge. The only solution to my predicament is to seek help, which, of course, I have done. You need to know it's okay to not be okay. I'll repeat what I wrote earlier: there are companies out there looking for veterans to hire. They are searching for people like you. All you need to do is to reach out and people will lift you up from that dark place you are in. You don't have to suffer something that can be helped, can be prevented. A simple online search might just bring you the help you need. There are also YouTube videos that will help with therapy. So if you are not comfortable exposing yourself out there, you can simply remain in the comfort of your home and receive the therapies you need. The only thing that may be required of you is personal discipline. You must be willing to change; otherwise, there is no point in seeking help. If you cannot bet on yourself, how do you expect other people to bet on you?

Age and Maturity

From a corporate point of view, I would advise young readers that it is never too late to fail. Yes, fail. In fact, failure is the best example of learning, and the more you fail the more it becomes a continuous process. Knowledge is fleeting. I want to address age and maturity in this next section. These two traits are mutually exclusive in few cases. In some situations, age does not constitute maturity. (I am not talking about physical maturity in this regard, but mental maturity.) A person can be old and still remain foolish. Indeed, there are fools at forty and geniuses at sixteen.

Still, wisdom resides with age in man to most cases. Never in a million years would I think that one of my best friends in the world would be a man in his seventies. He was old enough to be my grandfather but stood with me as a true friend. I came from a dysfunctional family, and my entire goal in life was to uproot my family tree and move it to better soil. To become a healthy and vibrant tree, not an ugly one mirroring its past.

There are various kinds of families. There are those that get along well and seem picture-perfect; they know about one another's challenges and try to find support for each other. Some of us are not blessed with these kinds of families, the traditional kinds of families that are law-abiding. There are some families that do not care about each other; with these units, it is almost every man for himself. They do not care how you survive or what you do to keep your head above water. In some ways, everything boils down to having a good family or bad family. You come from either one of them, good or bad—either way, there is nothing to be proud of or ashamed of. It is not your family's issues that will hold you back, but what you make of yourself. You can come from a bad situation and turn your life around, inspiring others to be good. That is what we truly lack in our modern day, the ability to call out bad people for what they are. Often we blanket-label the entire population for a few bad eggs. What really matters is the kind of person you choose to become. It's just like the philosophy that was ingrained in our Marine unit: it does not matter your race or where you come from, what matters is the kind of person you are.

As a young adult, it's not bad to seek the wisdom of elders. They are almost always ready to share their experiences to help you down the right path; that is, if you are ready to be pushed. You need real adult conversations in your life. There are some aspects of life that demand the knowledge of an elder; this knowledge will not let lead you astray. Your parents are probably the first people to have solid adult conversations with; they will most probably be relatable and willing to give you some of their nuggets of wisdom. They have probably gone through what you are going through, and they have learned the right choices to make. Therefore, it's a good thing to listen to them and follow their advice. However, if you don't have immediate family members who can give you this support (your parents are deceased or in no position to offer kind wisdom), you can try visiting your local McDonald's. And here, I am not joking. There you will find groups of old men with those old veterans hats on. All it takes is for you to walk up to them and have a polite conversation. They are always bored and tired of repeating the same things over and over, or telling lies to one another. So they will be happy to have your company, and they'll gladly give you all the weapons they have in their arsenal if you politely ask them. You never can tell what treasure is kept in those old heads. You cannot know until you try. Do not judge a book by its cover. Pick up the damn book and read a few pages before giving your final judgment.

It's a hard world we live in these days, a world where everyone thinks they get their fill of social interaction through social media. "I saw a picture and liked it." We now judge the state of a person through some fleeting pictures and videos, and we show our concern by "liking" them. That's a fake world, a fake persona. Rather than all of that, make the decision to meet with people off the social network and get to know who they truly are. Do not allow yourself to be swayed by all the flashy things being posted on the Internet. I do not know of anyone who has it all, who does not go through daily struggles. This is why you have to go to the root of things, to communicate with other human beings, especially folks who have seen it all. There is always something to be gained from them.

In doing this, you might discover that you were destined to do something else as opposed to what you think you should be doing. The revelation might open your eyes to lots of things, like changing your path. Your network will begin to grow because you're starting to talk to more people. And believe me, the power of having a strong network is incredible.

The best thing for me about being in sales is that I've now got people I know I can call on in every state in America, and international friends as well—sort of like the Marine Corps. We all come from different states and often very different places. And through having these people you've gathered in your network, you'll be able to have conversations that are fruitful. And if you listen to all these people, you will get the handiest skills ever, and you will learn to make the right choices because they have lived life and have great experience to share with you.

You just have to be a believer in learning from others and willing to ask questions. Then you will see them tell their stories—stories of regret and opportunities missed. From their mistakes might come your own opportunities. You just have to take a chance and walk up to them. Even now, I still receive words of wisdom from my dad as I take care of him. He has suffered a second stroke, and his quality of life is down.

If you look at someone older, especially someone who is terminally ill, one thing they are probably going to tell you as you listen to their stories is this: "I wish I would have done X, Y, and Z."

It is from their regrets that your own chance to be successful lies. Be wise and seek golden counsel from people willing to give it.

CHAPTER EIGHT

Time

Eventually you will run out of time.

Time is an asset we cannot make more of, and that's why it's so valuable. That's one big thing the war taught me; everyone's expiration date is inevitable. It would be great if we all knew what our time was. That way, we could properly prepare, but in reality we can never do that. So that's where perspective comes in with appreciating the now, because right now—these times that we're living in—this is all we have.

I wonder what would happen if you were told you had thirty days to live. I'm guessing you would not take another day for granted. You would not sit inside feeling sorry for yourself or honoring a lesser emotion because you'd want to live your last thirty days full of joy!

Time puts it all in focus. You're not going to worry, *Oh, I really missed that deadline at work*. And, *I should have done this or that*. Or, *maybe I could have made a little bit more money that year*.

None of that's going to matter. Yes, you'll eventually accept that it's your time. And you'll wish you would have had a little more time with those you care about. And it's the moments like right now—even during the pandemic of 2020-2021 and possibly beyond—that you gain perspective. You are probably living in some of the greatest times of your life; you just don't realize it yet. Distancing yourself from people you care about, things you like to do? Let's be real: it sucks. But I don't know another period in my life where I would have been at home working, earning a living, and with my family! For 14 months, 24/7 making memories. Special. That time has been invaluable to me. If you didn't get closer to your family over the first 365 days of the pandemic, that was a missed opportunity. That's what you're going to look back on in fifty years. History is a great teacher. Look back on your life for a brief time, where you have been, the low moments. You don't forget the feeling of those moments, but you certainly don't allow them to over-shadow the good times. History is also a great indication of what the future's going to hold. You still have time to change how you want the rest of your life to go. Depending on your current situation, the road ahead might be a lot of hard work, but *everything* in life is hard work.

Change your mind-set; appreciate every little thing and moment in life, because you're breathing—and life itself is so incredibly valuable. Life is hard. I haven't lost a parent or sibling yet. I'm grateful. What greater way of honoring those you love and care about, who have passed on, than simply living a good life?

There's no greater honor than that.

As I write this book, my father is ailing. His quality of life is not great. He can't see and is not mobile. I feel bad. It's a challenge seeing a parent go through that, and I don't know how, mentally, I'm going to prepare for that day. So I'm trying to live by the words I'm preaching, which is to just enjoy the moments I have left.

Spending more time with my family. That's one thing 2020 gave us.

When you spend time with the ones you love, it's a natural joy. Some of that time you don't even have to talk; you can just sit near them and listen.

There are people out there who are just built differently. We all play a role in society, but you can't knock a person when their tenacity and work ethic are superior to that of others. There are individuals who achieve greatness through obsession. It's easy to stand back and criticize or want another's lifestyle. The reality is, if you're not going to put that work in when nobody else is looking, if you are not willing to go farther than the competition, you aren't obsessed.

My goal is to become a great leader like that. I want to be invested in folks, listen to them, teach them it's family first. Where, if it's mid-morning and you need to run to a kid's recital or a graduation at preschool, I can tell the member of my team: go, we can cover for you, you belong there, in those moments, because that's what matters most.

Working for individuals who are terrible at leading others, who are selfish, who consider themselves fair, but they're biased—that's the worst. I've had a few of those in my life. My only advice for anyone working for someone like that: be gracious. They are setting you up for success by teaching you everything a leader is not.

Anger, like many other emotions, is difficult to control. I'm no different than any other human. My instincts to protect have been tempered by age and maturity, but when I see someone I care for being hurt or disrespected, my instincts to protect rise to the surface.

Discipline and repetition are two main ways to regulate negative emotions. To counteract the emotion, recognize the problem (show willingness to take criticism) and give yourself some leeway. It's normal for people to become enraged. To be honest, I don't get angry nearly as much as I used to. I've gone through various levels of learning, if you will, but I can still be very outspoken when I need be.

I'm also easily annoyed. For example, you come across people who say they only want positive vibes. "If you're not carrying the positive energy, don't talk to me!" What are we, a bunch of toddlers? That is the most arrogant and unrealistic statement I've ever heard. "Positive vibes only." Those types of folks are the most toxic because they're setting a dangerous expectation. Life is unpredictable, and it necessitates contemplation and a sense of gratitude for the present moment. But most importantly, it takes time.

If you ask me, children are the best life coaches. Everything inside of me changed when I became a father. If you want to call it something, call it a natural instinct. This tiny life form necessitates undivided attention and nurturing. It also necessitates discipline for your children to develop into their own unique, tiny human self. In general, children are cheerful, but there are moments when they become enraged and have tantrums. They also can be a blank slate. They don't hang on to hate or negativity. Usually those moments are over nearly as quickly as they come.

So how do you alter the poor habits? You can spank, timeout, or use a naughty rug—there are a plethora of parental rules and guidelines to choose from. For our family, the solution is right in front of us. This little guy needs a break, some time to relax, and you as a parent must calm him down. Children are the best teachers when it comes to learning to be a decent person. They haven't been exposed to the world's evil ways.

We're often too prideful as adults to know that changing our actions requires only a small amount of effort. Take a breather (if you can) if you're angry. There is obviously a lot of gray ground here, and different circumstances necessitate different approaches. Choose your battles carefully; not every situation that irritates you needs a call to action. Before saying something or responding in a way that can cause more pain, take a moment to calm down.

If you work remotely or communicate via email on a daily basis, here's a career-saving tip: create a rule in the settings to postpone the sending of your emails by a few minutes. That way, if you're having a rough day and come across a little short, you'll be prepared to make those changes. There is always time to change your attitude. Not everything requires an immediate response. If you know you are easily irritated, walk away—or better yet, sleep on it. Pick up the phone or have an in-person conversation. Do not type that stuff out; you leave typed words open to misinterpretation.

Recently, I underwent some testing at the VA. A question surfaced: "How often do you get angry?" My answer, in short, was: not very often. After further discussion, that was found to not be true. In my *mind*, I don't get angry.

Here I am thinking I'm in control of my feelings. The reality is, I'm not that strong. I get angry.

Mainly, this is because of irritability and other factors that can trigger a negative emotion for me. And, well, it's human nature. As much as I'd like to, I'm not sure I'm capable of just absorbing something and not reacting.

You may be irritated by someone or something. Learning to control emotions is a sign of maturity. But isn't that one of the benefits of growing up? Do you realize that having a negative effect on others—whether it's your children, a friend, or a family member—will hurt you and your current situation? How you treat yourself is everything. As a result, the faster you learn to deal with the negative circumstances, the better. I'm thankful the Marines put me in tough positions, that I was able to walk away and had learned critical life lessons. The reality is, this world is full of bad human beings. They're all around us. There is no piece of legislation or amendment out there that can change bad people. Yet society will try to pinpoint all the areas of opportunity—when the answer is directly in front of their faces. Bad people exist. They should be treated differently.

That's the protector mentality flowing out of me. One day when I was in my late twenties (no kids yet), I took my niece and nephew to McDonald's. I had them for a weekend and was just hanging out with them. My nephew was probably two or three at the time and was just enjoying the indoor play area. And there was this other older child in there being a bully. The bully child's parents were oblivious—until they met Uncle Josh. It was a very tense situation, as they carried the same mentality, as if they owned the area. Why did this moment stand out? Because I can't tolerate a bully. Growing up, my only desire in life was to have friends. That didn't come without trials and tribulations. I was picked on for my size, my body type, where we lived. Those encounters were necessary. Bullies are vital, if you ask me. It produced in me a sort of fight.

What's crazy is I've been around guys who are stone-cold killers—badasses who are the cream of the crop. Guys who are capable of ending a life yet are more humble and kind than someone walking around acting the part. You know the type. Some of the guys I served with have the biggest hearts. They're loving. They signed on the line to give up their life for complete strangers. They want to change the world for the better. Please do not take their kindness as weakness. If those types are willing to lay down their own life for strangers, imagine the lengths they'll go to fight for their own.

Criticism is a tough pill to swallow. I don't know anyone who enjoys it. But in my experience, that type of feedback is necessary. Humble yourself to accept the good with the bad. It all comes down to willingness and, ultimately, sacrifice in order for someone to effectively change behaviors.

Perhaps you're stuck. Perhaps you've put yourself in a financial bind that will prevent you from making the necessary changes right away. That's fine.

However, committing to the needed change will necessitate an immediate sacrifice. Nothing worthwhile is ever achieved without an equal amount of hard work and sacrifice.

Here are some examples.

Need to lose weight? Hard work and sacrifice—both are required.

Do you want to get ahead at work or in school? Both attributes are required.

Determine your pain points and concentrate on eliminating behaviors that are holding you back. Make a sacrifice.

What are you willing to give up? You have to be able to self-inventory and figure out your gaps. It's easy to have goals. But what do you lack? Embracing the realities and difficulties of your individual gaps is critical to success.

There is plenty of support literature and information out there you can get your hands on without spending any money. Today you can find tons of motivation or assistance on YouTube if you want to work out or do something and learn from other people. I have checked off some boxes in life, but in no way am I content. I'm obsessed with becoming a better version of myself.

So it's back to the basics for me. Just listening, listening to others, and, more importantly, listening to myself, trying to figure out what it is I truly want to achieve in life. That so-called pursuit of happiness. I've decided that I don't know if my life will allow me to be truly happy. I don't think that exists for me. It's not because I have gone without love or I need anything. These things going on in my head are exhausting. They cripple emotion. This doesn't mean I am giving up; I have too much fight to allow that to happen. But it's difficult to explain the type of numbness I have within.

Jim always talked about becoming debt free and not having to owe anyone. Maybe your goals are different. My service to the country unlocked levels of suck that make my normal day-to-day seem like a cakewalk. Again: perspective.

Sometimes it just means getting out of your comfort zone, and if that comfort zone is living in the same town you've lived in your entire life, maybe it means packing up and moving somewhere else where you don't know anyone. And that's a huge risk factor, but again, you're drowning yourself with negative people or people who will constantly just keep you down, within that status quo. If you're not constantly looking for new people who provide inspiration, you need to take a very real inventory of who you have around you. In terms of inspiration, my circle has changed a hundred times in the last ten years. And it only comes from exposure and meeting new people. That is the power of human capital. Don't let the media or social outlets deter you, creating in you the thinking that the world is coming to a close. Get back out there and see other people in their natural habitat. The light will always shine greater than the dark. That is why, if anyone asks me, "Why do you love sales," my answer comes back to: it always comes down to people. I love good people. Listening to what drives them, what they enjoy, how they became who they are. It's fascinating to me.

My biggest weakness right now is my lack of a spiritual home. Growing up, the women in my life were heavily involved in our small church. A southern Baptist church is where I learned who God was. I understand the power of faith and certainly have called out for help when I most need it. I like to think we have a unique relationship. However, I also think: who am I kidding?

I recall when I was paid five dollars an hour to work forty hours per week scrubbing toilets and mowing grass, putting in long hours and earning two hundred dollars per week. Things are different now. For instance, take materialistic things— it's easy to think on the surface level—as if all the "things" will make you happy. "If I make six figures, I'll be . . . I'll be different." The truth is you are not unique. The money and objects are not important. It's the people you interact with on a daily basis. That is my joy, knowing that I can continue to improve their lives and the lives of my other family members. However,

I believe a real faith must be organically introduced into the mix. And, truthfully, that's probably where a lot of our family's problems surfaced from, once we got away from the church.

There are a million different ways to self-improve, and yet I've overlooked the most important message. In the Bible we all have access to the oldest, truest form of life education put in one book. Think about it. I mean, every aspect that we struggle with is discussed in that book, and whether you agree with it or not, faith is powerful. In Iraq, I carried a Bible in my cargo pocket, and I found Scriptures that were immediately helpful. You draw strength from it, you draw inspiration.

We had someone who came around and prayed for us. I always participated. They have Catholic prayer circles and Protestant circles, as far as I recall, even in boot camp. And I'm just bouncing around from night to night, trying to figure out where . . . *what* . . . message I'm supposed to be receiving. I can recall this older gentleman in boot camp. He was mid-thirties and just had a way of bringing calm to the chaos. He was mature. Odd how that happens, huh? I tend to always gravitate toward the older and more experienced; they just hit me differently. I mean, here's a guy who's in his early thirties, on the verge of 35, aging out of the military. He was also overweight and balding. You could tell he was slower than the majority of the teenagers in boot camp with him. But man, when he spoke about his life and experience, so many younger guys were drawn to his ability to teach. Whether you believe or not is entirely your business, but I would say this: there are plenty of examples of how faith turned people's lives around. That has gained my attention.

One of the things about this book that has me excited is the ability to speak to the youth of America. To share more experiences. Having a 16-year-old, much younger sister has taught me a lot about the mind-set of today's youth. They desire and seek instant gratification. They want the big house, six figures, nice cars, and a job that does not put them to the test.

My advice to anyone younger who wants to make the most of their life? Slow the F down. This isn't a knock, so please deflate the chest a bit. We were young once too, and I can assure you I didn't know anything back then. I thought I did. In hindsight, I would have lived with my mom a while longer. I would have not opted for a car payment, but instead invested my money.

Why rush into a life of hardship? The great thing about being young is that no one, and I mean no one, has any expectations of you—only you do. You've got time on your side. To be honest, there is no age limit for this message. Take these things to heart instead of dwelling and clinging to this fictitious expectation of what life should be.

* * * * *

Take this moment to write down what you want out of life. Go ahead. Maybe even write it here:

_____

_____

_____

Also, make a note of this somewhere important to you. Don't give yourself a deadline, either; dreams don't expire. Some simply take a little longer to materialize. Start small if necessary. I'm not expecting you to run a marathon. When you start checking things off your list, you're learning to appreciate even the smallest of victories. *That* is a lovely thing. Learn to celebrate and appreciate the wins, no matter how big or small.

Now for a bit more sound advice. Have faith in the wisdom of the elderly. When did we stop encouraging people to respect their elders? Have you ever heard someone say, "Man, if I only knew what I know now and could go back . . . "? There's a lot of truth in that. I didn't know anything back in the day. I was so proud of myself, puffing my chest out; nothing was going to stop me mentally. "We're not going to war, Mom!" I said. Well, my ass went off to a very real war. It's admirable to believe that once you graduate high school or college your life will go as planned. At such a young age, to have it all figured out. Truer words have never been written, but life will always find a way to humble you.

Let's shift gears from the doom and gloom. I'm certainly not trying to thwart your vision or plans. I'm just trying to help you understand, to see some basic things. Things will work out, you will be fine; just enjoy the ride. Open your mind to those who are older than you or have been in your shoes. We understand: you want it all, and we did too. Take advantage of your twenties to learn more about yourself. That is: go out and fail. Work hard at something and fall flat on your face a couple of times. That's not a bad thing! Why is this so? Those moments are teachers. And you have time on your side. You can make those kinds of mistakes because you aren't expected to have everything figured out just yet.

Life has gotten better for me as I've gotten older. However, improvements in the quality of life necessitated an equal amount of time, failure, success, learning, and hard work. I had to work for the life I desired, and guess what? I'm still not where I want to be. Even now, I'm taking applications for new friendships. New teachers. Despite my anxiety and mental hurdles about what could go wrong, I recognize that having those interactions with others, the conversations and friendships, are enriching my life.

If you want to increase your net worth, you must constantly improve your network. The people you're surrounded by. For the first time in twenty years I don't have my most trusted sounding board. Jim was the guy I turned to for advice. Fortunately, his nuggets of wisdom are ingrained in my DNA, and now it's up to me to teach the next generation, or anyone willing to listen.

The goal of this book, for me, is significant. I truly want to immerse myself in these things, to surround myself with greatness. People are motivating. From the CEO to the person scrubbing toilets, all of us can benefit from being open to the unique message of another person. Use their teachings to reach a new audience and give other people hope. We all came from somewhere; we were all blank slates once. And as we've spun around on this massive rock through space, our paths have often crossed. But there is good to be found, a story to be told, and if you allow yourself to be open to learning, exploring, and enjoying other people, you can lead a great life as well.

CHAPTER NINE

Get Better Today

War never leaves you. We all face battles in our life, engagements of varying magnitude. Nothing will ever compare, for me, to that war. I mean that, for most of my adult life since, I've been isolated in a kind of silence. Imagine the best and worst thing to ever happen to you, and then isolating those things deep into the semi-forgotten. This is for anyone who has been through a battle you think you cannot overcome.

A piece of me will always be over there, my spirit forever intertwined with the chaos of that place. That war.

Only those who have firsthand experience in combat truly understand that statement. But that doesn't mean conflicts aren't still raging in our lives. The war on the mind is unceasing. Just as you are built to withstand the events of tomorrow with resilience and grit, it's okay to acknowledge a defeat. That war was singlehandedly the best and worst thing to ever happen to me. It made me tough and fearless in my work, but it also made me fearful and lonely on the inside. Numb. Closed off. Distant.

That doesn't mean you have to accept a defeat and consider it permanent. Enemies both internal and external are banking on that acceptance. Your life is far too precious to those who care about you to give up. We all were brought into this world the same way. We are all sons or daughters. Which is why you need to start slow as you begin your healing process. Crawl if you have to.

Persistence is always greater than resistance. It's that hidden frequency within the subconscious that learns to adapt and overcome to what's currently around you today. Accept that for both good and bad. Begin to make small adjustments to gain a better perspective.

That's today's benchmark. Hell, you may need to rest a while longer; you may need to seek help from someone stronger who can help you out of this emotional rut. But at some point you have to begin fighting for yourself again. Each day raising that bar until you are accomplishing things you couldn't yesterday. Take the walk. Take the trip. Feel the sun on your face. None of us are making it out of this alive, so why are we wasting the time we have? There are plenty of reminders around us that should motivate us to get better. If you can't find the motivation or the time—hey, I call bullshit. Everyone is given the same amount of time in a day. The difference is how you are managing that time. Find time to walk every day and connect with nature, or work on yourself by putting down those things such as personal screens that we depend on, and make the time. Change your habits. Set an alarm. Make your bed. (I've said this, but want to say it again; it's important. I can't tell you how much more improved my day is when my bed is made. I love military edges, too, tight corners, where you can bounce a quarter or a recruit's head off of it.)

Why is it, when we are years down the road, we finally appreciate the life we had *then*? The people we were around then. Life is so precious, and thankfully the war has given me that understanding. I am able to appreciate the moment. Doesn't mean I'm perfect in that ideology, but, for the most part, I realize the blessing and try to do more good than harm.

Learn to appreciate and celebrate the small incremental victories. Bottle those small victorious times up and save them. Things in the rear view, while important, are smaller in scope since they are already behind you. Everything in front of you, right now, is more important.

But also, understand that you *will* hit that setback. Those are okay; nobody is perfect 100 percent of the time. I call this living within my relative expectation. It's so hard to not get distracted. Trust me. I want, crave, and yearn for more of that feeling.

But again, keep the understanding that persistence will prevail. That is what my life has taught me. It's that mind-set that I must work for everything that has gotten me to where I am today. Persistence. Jim loved perpetual motion, the act of never stopping. Move or die.

Even when you aren't moving, you can still be moving ahead in your thought process. Reading a book, seeking out videos online, or calling that trusted advisor or friend. That's power that you can go get. The greatest people you know have that mind-set. They don't have all the answers; they take calculated risks.

* * * * *

Instead of wanting the best of everything or anyone, learn to appreciate what you have going on today. Seeing death in Iraq taught me that. Don't go chasing the reaper. But also, sometimes, if you tiptoe that line, you'll find out when you are really living.

Example: take a big inhale of oxygen. Hold that for a few seconds, then exhale. Repeat as many times as necessary. That feeling right there. That is you, *living*. There are graveyards full of white crosses who fought for you. You are absolutely special, so quit acting like your situation is worse than anyone else's. You have the foundation of life to build on. Coincidentally, in my search for happier days, it turns out that breathing is the first step to controlling anxiety and fears. Those two realizations are all you need to begin your journey. Think about it. If you are capable of taking a breath right now, you have already won the battle of the day. Appreciate it and stay in the fight, my friends.

It's hard for me to imagine achieving success without leaning on the support of others. Growing up, it was about leaning on friends and family, then entering into athletics where you had a team. Everyone played a role, and you learned to work hard together, learned to win and lose. Fast-forward to the Marines: we do not leave one another behind. That doesn't mean that we agree or get along with one another 100 percent of the time, but we do have each other's back.

There are objectives in boot camp that challenge you both individually and as a team, and everyone contributes equally. It's important. Sure, a Marine is trained as a deadly marksman, capable of winning on the battlefield. But imagine hundreds if not thousands of those hard chargers, in unison, staring at you down range. It's that *esprit de corps,* that bond, that brotherhood that kept me alive. It's that same energy that is keeping me in the fight today. It's tough being alone, or feeling that isolation, like you cannot talk to someone for clarity. And, in the civilian sector, you are going to encounter individuals who do not have the same work ethic, the same team mentality.

I heard something the other day that was so relative to the leader I hope to become. I don't own a business yet, but I work hard for the owners who employ me. Always have. I have a deep level of appreciation and respect. Not everyone who works with you has that same mentality or desire; not everyone has bought in. Guess what? That's okay. It's okay for executives to work harder than their employees. Why? They are the owners, they are vested; it's their vision, their blood, sweat, and tears, their brand. The best leaders understand and appreciate everyone's contribution. We are all unique; no two are the same. So if you have an employee who wants to just show up for forty hours and then go home? Embrace them. There are people out there who only want that. Don't punish them for that mentality or judge them. A good leader will simply appreciate the job they are tasked with and make sure they're getting it completed. If serving is beneath you, then leadership is beyond you. Anyone can become successful or accomplished. You have the ability to achieve your heart's desires, but you will learn that those achievements do not define you personally. Achievements can leave you empty and heartless; a true leader never puts those things over those around them.

I have some amazing friends and family, folks I can always depend on. I am fortunate to have my Marines with me too. However, I would be lying if I said I hadn't wasted much time in personal isolation. I am different. Don't know if I will ever be 100 percent again in that regard, in terms of my struggles with PTSD.

It's simply exhausting. But this book project has given me courage again, and it has also reopened communication with the boys. Marines are built differently. They are there when I need them regardless of the downtime in between, and that's powerful. I'm learning that the Veterans Administration has wonderful programs and a community of warriors looking to help. You just have to take the ownership and seek it out.

Time is relative, perhaps the only constant. Have you ever looked into the eyes of a person who is running out of time? Generally older people, or someone who is gravely ill. They are filled with so much emotion, both good and bad, and some are regrets: *wish I would have told them I loved them more . . . wish I could have done this differently . . . wish I would have treated myself with better care.*

We still have time to fix those things. It's right here.

* * * * *

So how do you get better today? Obviously there are levels and differences to everyone's scope. For me, I have often sought out someone around me to learn from. I lucked out with Jim. I lucked out having two really strong and independent parents and siblings. That doesn't mean that the suffering or struggles have ceased, but it's a combination of combined experiences that matters.

Jim had 98 years on this earth, a marriage spanning more than sixty years, a world war, the Great Depression, and a life-long commitment to one company under his belt. He had two children who he cared for immensely, and they felt his love and understanding. Having someone you can ask questions of, who can teach you and mold you; this is so invaluable. I cannot wait to teach my sons or share with anyone willing to listen.

My family and friends have also been supportive and understanding of my path. Each has endured countless heartache and setbacks of their own, but accountability matters. It's kept me going.

If you are looking for or are in search of a mentor or someone to learn from, my advice is to start with someone in plain sight. Start with your inner circle. Ask your parents questions. Not just any questions. Tough life questions. Chances are you will be surprised at the similarities. Go up to the older people at the local breakfast spot. Older people will tell it to you straight and unfiltered. Deep questions, and they can relate to your struggles. They'll really listen. You are likely to find some great information. Listening is one of the handiest skill sets anyone can learn. Unadulterated, full, undivided attention. Those types of genuine encounters are intoxicating.

From there, challenge yourself at work to seek out someone who heads a department you have interest in. Interview them, take them to lunch. Ask for the job, or how to get to that job. Soak in everything, and then begin to apply that over and over until you are recognized as the hungriest person in the room, someone they would be dumb to overlook. Work is important to me. I value my work. The work I put in has never let me down. Anytime I needed something, it's the work that created the opportunity to advance my position.

* * * * *

Don't be afraid to take calculated risks. I know: that's easier said than done. But I can't preach this enough. You have to prepare for setbacks and critiques. Time on this earth has afforded me that ability of reflection. I would love to, as they say, "start over with the knowledge I have today." I could have gotten a head start on the person I hope to be one day. But we aren't going to live with regrets. Nope. We are going to take the necessary steps forward and learn to appreciate the path along the way.

One of the messages I'd like you to take upon reading this book is that you truly can make the decision to get better—starting today. When I was writing this book and brainstorming titles with the team, we kicked around several. One was *Get Better Today.*

For me, it's relatable in the sense that I took chances, understood the mission at hand in hopes of improving every life situation, and never gave up. Perseverance is never giving up despite your emotional state, because no one said you won't have bad days.

The hardest thing anyone can do in life is admit fault or admit being wrong. Often, people want to try to figure it out on their own, and they end up refusing help. Often the best way to get ahead in life is to fail, or learn, or both. Every bad day is just *a* (single) bad day. It's not you, it's not your life, and it's not your future. It's just one bad day in a sea of thousands. The sun is coming up tomorrow. Make a plan to change your scenery to achieve better tomorrows if you feel the day was a waste. Don't get down on yourself. Just make a new plan.

Did you get better today? If not, let's get to work!

* * * * *

Part of my plan for this book is donating proceeds to veterans' charities, or maybe this will lead to the creation of my own nonprofit for those struggling with PTSD, and not just veterans. I want this to be more than a book. I want you to have a tool for your belt, a reminder that you are not alone.

Never give up, because you have what it takes to beat any bad day. All you have to do is focus on putting one foot in front of the other. And, once more: take this moment to stop being so hard on yourself. Most of the time we tend to get too ahead of ourselves, with thinking, planning, or worry—or too far behind, by looking back. When we look back, or ahead, we completely miss the moment!

Let's all try to stay in this moment a while longer. You have folks behind you, folks on your six.

CONCLUSION

Find Your Cadence

Today is the day to start working on getting better no matter how you might feel.

How can I overcome this challenge set before me to become an even greater version of myself?

Sometimes it's simply a daily battle between our ears.

Focus on the steps it's going to take; focus on the cadence. When you are marching down this path, this life, find the cadence you hope to follow: left foot, right foot . . . the cadence will be different for everyone. Everyone is built differently. I can remember being so tired, but I knew, in order to claim the title, to achieve my goal, I had to give more. I could see the end, the top of the mountain, and I dreaded the pain ahead. It sucked.

When it's time, you are either going to make it or you are going to learn.

I learned a lot during my time in the military.

The cadence, and the tempo, can and will change. That's to be expected, and I also learned that sometimes in life you have to do an about-face, and that's a setback.

Or at least it seems that way at the time. How many times in life did you face a setback and turn around and things ended up better than the direction you were originally going in?

It's okay to reset the pace, even to change directions. But it's important to remember what got you there, and how you felt, and learn to embrace the suck. Don't get me wrong; I hate those cheesy statements. "Embrace the suck." Or, "Pain is weakness leaving the body." Complete cringe. And yet, there are some truths there. It's pain that generates a response, and that is your fight-or-flight mentality. Marines are taught to move forward, change tempo, and, as long as you're breathing, you are still in the fight. That mentality can be used daily in your journey to find your greater moment. My advice is to get back in rhythm with your life, find your true cadence, and decide it's time to conquer your battle of the day.

Sometimes you'll be inspired to take giant leaps. At other times, it's just a step.

If you think about it, everything occurs with one step, whether it's a child going from infant to walking, or a team training to work together for the first time, or even completing a 5K or marathon.

Whatever any human goal is, it begins with that first step. (But then, that's not enough, right?)

Each day you've got to make the decision to take another step. And another step. And another . . .

Ultimately, the biggest decision you make will be to take that first step. What do you do when you can't? Call, text, reach out for help. I have been blessed to have served with, or lucked into friendships with, some of the finest humans this earth has to offer. This book pays homage to where I have been, this journey, my service in the United States Marines, and becoming a combat veteran of the Iraq Invasion of 2003. And, as well, all the challenges of a war, and those hidden scars that remained long after. This book represents my newfound mission in life, to share my pain and struggles with hopes to heal, and to give back to those deserving, much like those who gave to me.

Right now you are living in some of your greatest days—and you most likely haven't realized it yet. It's human nature to view what's in our past as being our best days. Those days only hold the highest value because we captured the moment. Perhaps you are a dreamer and feel as if tomorrow, or years down the road, will be better. I am here to share with you that today will always be better than yesterday, and more meaningful than tomorrow.

Today my goals are simple: get up, get after it, and be thankful for the greatness you are about to achieve. Sometimes you won't be able to do it on your own. You cannot allow yourself to be defeated by an invisible enemy in your mind.

Find your cadence. Start. The march begins.

THE AUTHOR AND THE MESSAGE OF THIS BOOK

Joshua W. White is a combat veteran who served during the 2003 invasion of Iraq. His story of what it's like growing up in a fly-over state, riddled with poverty and drugs, and how the Marine Corps calling changed his life forever, is a story we all need to hear. *Among the Greatest* is a real-life testimonial from the front lines of a major U.S. conflict—and the struggle to readjust back into society as a young man. For any person who is suffering with Post-Traumatic Stress Disorder, or who lives with daily adversity, this is a testament to weathering the toughest storms and putting yourself back to work.

The hardest thing anyone can do is admit their mistakes, accept something is wrong, and recognize they need help. It's important to share that, even during the toughest of days, there are lessons to be learned within the chaos. It's those lessons that lead to some of the greatest outcomes in life. As long as you are breathing, you are still in the fight. You can still make a difference. Now, let's get to work.